Gardener's Handbook 1

Broad-leaved Trees

David Carr

B. T. BATSFORD LTD, LONDON

First published 1979
© David Carr 1979
ISBN 0 7134 1305 0

Filmset in VIP Times by Elliott Bros. & Yeoman Ltd,
Speke, Liverpool L24 9JL
Printed by The Anchor Press Ltd,
Tiptree, Essex
for the publishers B. T. Batsford Ltd,
4 Fitzhardinge Street, London W1H 0AH

Gardener's Handbook 1
Broad-leaved Trees

Contents

List of trees

Botanical name

English popular names

American popular names

Introduction

Most people would consider the growing of trees to be a long-term venture, yet it is often embarked upon almost on the spur of the moment, to satisfy some whim or fancy. When some trees, like oaks, have a life span many times that of man, a certain amount of forethought makes sense.

The aim of this book is to greatly increase the chances of successfully selecting the right tree for a site when planting afresh. The art of good cultivation consists of: correctly assessing the various aspects of a site, its climate and soil; then choosing plants to suit both site and intended purpose; and finally by good cultural practice, ensuring that plant needs are met. With increasing pollution, the modern tendency towards smaller gardens and the greater availability of trees from foreign parts, the matter of choice of trees becomes of even greater importance than before.

This book consists of two parts: the first covers various aspects of planting and tree care; in the second part descriptions of some trees of garden merit and their requirements are given.

List of colour plates

The fresh spring foliage of Japanese Maple and *Acer pseudoplatanus* 'Brilliantissimum'

Robinia pseudoacacia 'Frizia' displaying the beauty of individual leaves

Spring colouring in greens, golds and purple

Purple-leaved *Prunus* 'Pissardii', Willow-leaf Pear and *Robina* 'Frizia' in summertime

The spring glory of Common Horse Chestnut and Red Chestnut

Japanese Maple demonstrating its autumn tints

A summer-long succession of colour by *Catalpa bignonioides* 'Aurea'

The summer flowers of the Tulip Tree

Photographs supplied by kind permission of Harry Smith, horticultural photographic collection.

Planting trees

The factors which influence plant growth and development in any garden are: climate; nature of site; soil; biological influences; time; and the attention of the cultivator.

Climate and location

Plants and trees are described as hardy where they can survive outdoors. Those which are quite hardy in mild southern conditions may not survive in more northern districts. Climate, the combined and cumulative effects of sun, wind, frost and rain, imposes certain characteristics on a region or place and its vegetation. For example, given protection from prevailing winds the climate in coastal districts is usually cooler in summer and warmer in winter than that of inland areas.

Site

On a smaller scale, in a sheltered garden some plant or tree can flower weeks before another of the same type in an exposed position in the same neighbourhood. Sunny, south-facing slopes, protected from cold north or east winds, are the warmest, most favoured sites.

Shade is another limiting factor for some trees, as are buildings, plot size and altitude.

Soils

Soils vary according to their chemical and physical composition and trees, like other plants, show preferences for certain soil types.

One of the most important single factors is soil reaction – the degree of acidity or alkalinity – which can be expressed or measured against the pH scale. This is a unit system in which a pH of 7 is neutral, numbers less than 7 are acid and those above are alkaline. Soil pH can be tested either by analysts, or at home using an inexpensive soil testing kit, which can be obtained from garden centres or hardware stores. For example, Mountain Ash grows best on acid soil; the presence of chalk or limestone usually indicates neutral or alkaline conditions, which are preferred by trees such as Beech.

Fertile soils contain essential plant nutrients including nitrogen, phosphates, potash and other elements. It is also important that they should be free-draining.

The physical qualities of soil vary greatly according to the respective quantities of clay and sand present. Clay soils are sticky and heavy when wet and rock-hard when dry. Sandy soils are gritty to the touch, free-draining and easier to cultivate. The most productive soils are blends of clays and sands, suitably fertilized and limed if necessary, and are termed loams.

Biological influences

Plants and animals act and react with each other to cause various effects. In a natural wood, for example, there are often thin, narrow, spindly trees which, because of the unequal competition with others, have not been able to develop properly. In a garden it is important to allow trees adequate space to grow and develop.

Again, if we consider the levels of vegetation in a woodland setting, there are at least three or four. Trees provide the topmost canopy, and, depending on the amount of light to reach the lower and ground levels, the nature and extent of the undergrowth will vary. The lower layers of vegetation consist of the woodland floor plants, which roughly correspond to the herbaceous plants, grasses and low ground cover subjects of gardens. The intermediate layer of scrub, between floor and overhead canopy, has its counterpart in garden shrubs. Each of these layers competes against the others for food, light and moisture, factors to be considered when planting. Last, but by no means least of the plants, are members of the micro-flora – the mosses, lichens, fungi and others. Some of these live by growing on our cultivated plants and cause disease.

Birds and animals, especially members of the insect world, also exert considerable influence on the success or failure of our trees. Caterpillars, which devour vast quantities of leaves, are among the more destructive, and steps to control them are occasionally necessary.

Time
This is a very significant dimension, especially where the cultivation of trees is involved. We are concerned with plants not only in the present but for some years ahead, changing and growing in size and stature – another point to be considered when planting. Therefore consider the ultimate height and spread, not forgetting the depth and breadth of root systems, in relation to the surroundings.

The attention of the cultivator
The aims of a good gardener should be: to select and plant the tree or trees best suited to the site; to provide good growing conditions; and to attend to the needs of plants, training and pruning as and when necessary. Factors affecting the selection of trees are considered in detail in the individual descriptions in the second part of the book. Before considering the nature and methods of the cultural operations involved in tree growing, some indication of their requirements may be helpful.

Requirements for growth
Each of the factors given below plays an important role in the life of a tree. Some of these we can control, others we can influence only to a limited extent.

Temperature is one of the most powerful factors – growth of many hardy trees virtually ceases below about 6°C (42°F) and increases rapidly with greater warmth. Leaves, shoots, roots and buds can be damaged at around –1°C (30°F) in late spring when growth is advanced. The precise level at which low temperatures damage plants or trees depends on their hardiness, the season and their condition. Trees can be classed in descending order of hardiness, A, B, and C, which relate to climatic zones (Figs. 1a and 1b).

Water, especially soil moisture, and air are of the utmost importance

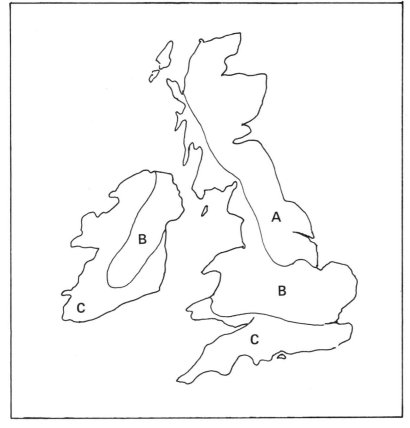

Figure 1a
Great Britain

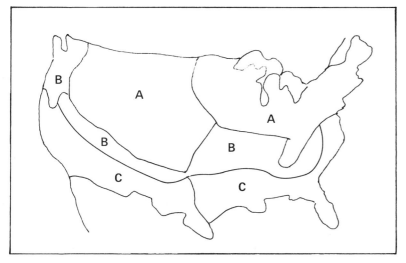

Figure 1b
North America
Climatic zones:
    A = cool temperate
    B = mild temperate
    C = warm temperate
N.B. The terms used here are for the purpose of this book and are not exact from a purely geographical viewpoint. High ground, exposed or north-facing sites fall into cooler classification.

to the survival, growth and development of trees.

Too much or too little water can be fatal. Roots can extract essential plant nutrients from the ground only when they are dissolved in a diluted watery solution. Excess water for long periods results in suffocation of tree roots and death.

Sunlight is vitally important to trees and their development. Light is, of course, necessary for plants to manufacture sugars and starches by means of chlorophyll in their leaves, without which growth would

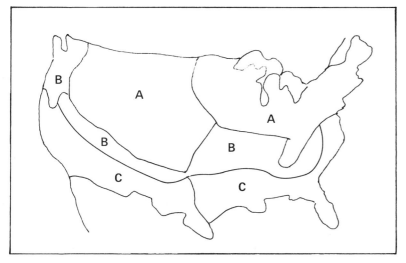

13

cease. But as not all sites are in full sun, it is necessary to know which varieties either need, or can tolerate light shade.

Another important requirement is adequate space to grow. Overcrowding results in weak, spindly disease-prone growth. Trees, planted too close to buildings and drains, can damage foundations in various ways and cause blockage due to root action.

Finally it is important to consider the effects of pollution, especially when planting in towns. Pollution in towns has many harmful effects – it causes soil acidity from sulphur deposits; salt spray from roads; fumes and deposits affecting plant processes. Many deciduous trees can tolerate a higher level of pollution than evergreens.

Selecting trees

In selecting a tree both the needs of the gardener (namely, will the tree serve its purpose?) and the requirements of the tree have to be taken into consideration.

In present-day gardens trees, other than those grown for fruit, are required primarily for decorative purposes, but also serve to provide shelter and screening. When selecting trees for screens take care to choose a variety that is sufficiently hardy for the purpose in mind. For example, in an exposed position wind can cause considerable disfiguration of tender trees.

The natural habit of shape or outline of trees can provide considerable scope for variety and interest in any garden layout. There are five basic forms or outlines of tree shape, and these are briefly discussed below.

Fastigiate trees are tall or upright and narrow in proportion to their height, *Sorbus* hybrida 'Fastigiata' is an example of this type.

Pyramidal forms are conical in outline, broader at the base, narrowing and tapering towards the top. Malus tschonoskii is one of the best examples of this shape.

Upright trees can take various forms, but the type, such as *Robinia pseudoacacia* grows roughly twice as high as broad.

Globose or round-headed forms are common among deciduous trees. Thorns and some of the Maples are common examples of this group.

The last basic group consists of weeping trees. Willows and Birch are common examples, but many species of deciduous trees have a weeping form.

Other important considerations are colour and season of interest. Some trees, such as Eucalyptus and Evergreen oaks, can provide year-round colour with their foliage. Others, among them Silver Birch and some Cherries and Maples, have attractive bark or stems.

The autumn leaf colouring of some trees can be more effective than their flowers and fruits, as is frequently found among Maples.

Fruits and berries can not only extend the season of colour into autumn and winter, but also provide food for birds and animals, and so add more interest.

Buying trees

This aspect of selection should include some thought about the size and condition of the tree being obtained, as well as the variety. This in turn depends to some extent on the planting season.

The conventional period for moving deciduous trees – those which shed their leaves in autumn – into their final position is after the leaves have fallen, and before growth recommences in spring. For most trees of this group, planting during autumn, winter and early spring is usual.

The forms in which trees can usually be obtained are summarized in the following list.

Whips or transplants: young nursery stock with a single stem or a feathered single stem – one which has a number of short growths or shoots. These can vary in height from about 300mm (1ft) to 1.5m (5ft) or more. However, this form requires careful pruning to build up a good framework of branches. Certain trees, Parrotia and Paulownia, for example, are best moved when fairly small, usually up to about 1.2m (4ft) high.

Bush trees: a framework of branches on a short main stem, usually 300–750mm (1–2½ft) from ground to lowest branch.

Half-standard and full-standard trees: similar to bush forms except that the main stem or trunk is longer, 1–1.4m (3½–4½ft) and 1.7–2m (5½–7ft) respectively.

Two other forms of tree are sometimes offered for sale.

Extra-heavy nursery stock: trees which have been grown on for an extra year or two and have a better developed framework of branches and roots as well as thicker stems. This grade is usually confined to deciduous trees.

Semi-mature, large deciduous trees: occasionally available, but their high cost and extra care needed for success do not make them a particularly attractive proposition. Their chief advantage is immediate effect.

Trees can be prepared in the following ways as regards treatment of the roots.

Bare-root trees: with all the soil removed. This treatment is adequate for some varieties of deciduous trees, provided they are small trees; do not dry out; and are lightly pruned immediately after planting.

Balled trees: with a ball of soil around the roots.

Balled-and-wrapped (b-a-w) trees: with the root ball wrapped in hessian or similar, to prevent the soil from working loose. This method, when carefully carried out, works well for most kinds of tree.

Container-grown trees: grown in some form of receptacle. Trees so treated can be planted out at almost any time of year, provided the ground is not frozen, waterlogged or baked hard.

The following table sets out in summary form the factors to be borne in mind when buying trees for a garden.

Figure 2
1 Fastigiate
2 Pyramidal
3 Globose or round
4 Upright or columnar
5 Weeping

Tree habit
1 Fastigiate
2 Pyramidal
3 Globose or round } any of which can be combined with the following permutations
4 Upright
5 Weeping

Tree form
1 Whips or transplants, including feathered
2 Bush
3 Half-standard
4 Standard
5 Extra-heavy stock
6 Semi-mature

Tree root condition
1 Bare root
2 Balled
3 Balled-and-wrapped
4 Container-grown

Other considerations
Purpose of planting
Ultimate size, height, width and rootrun
Rate of growth
Nature of interest: leaves, flowers, fruits, etc.
Season of attraction
Hardiness
Tree needs, of site and soil
Cultural requirements, pruning and training

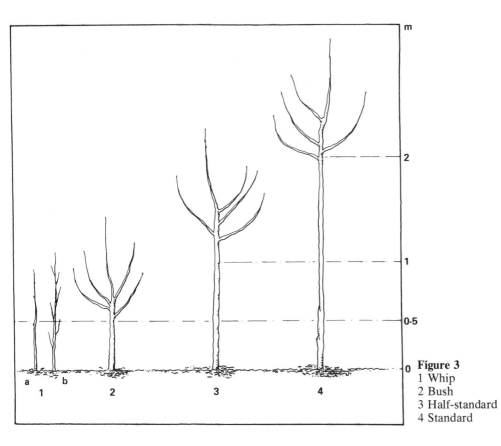

Figure 3
1 Whip
2 Bush
3 Half-standard
4 Standard

Figure 4
1 Bare root
2 Balled
3 Balled-and-wrapped
4 Container grown

Cultural requirements

For best results these tasks should be carried out in a logical sequence. If we take as our starting point an uncultivated site, the sequence of operations can be considered under a number of stages.

Site preparation

First the site should be cleared of all weeds and rubbish. Dig out perennial weeds like nettles, thistles and docks. If the land is literally choked with weed, it may be better to defer planting and apply a weedkiller such as 2,4,5,–T or 2,4,–D. Take care not to kill more plants than intended. The ground should be clear of any injurious chemical residues before planting can safely take place. The time the soil is left before planting depends on rainfall, soil type, the nature and amount of herbicide used. Follow the makers' instructions.

Land drainage should be checked and if necessary attended to. This may entail installing pipe drainage or some other means of disposing of surplus water.

Any changes to ground levels should be made before planting, when it is both quicker and easier.

The area around the immediate planting excavation should be cultivated to a spade depth and some manure or similar material incorporated.

Preparation for planting

Excavate a hole at least 600mm (2ft) square and as deep, keeping the good topsoil on one side but removing clay or poor subsoil. Where trees which have a large root ball are to be planted, increase the size to at least 300mm (1ft) wider and deeper than the size of the root mass.

Fork up the bottom of the hole, and incorporate one bucketful of peat or well rotted manure plus 120g (4oz.) of bonemeal to an area of 600 × 600mm (2 × 2ft).

Hammer in a suitable support where necessary, before planting. Timber stakes should be debarked, and treated with an approved safe preservative. The stake, say 40mm (1½in.) square, should be of sufficient length so that the top is about 50mm (2in.) below the lowest branches of half-standards and standards, or two-thirds the height of bush or small trees, and the bottom is 300mm (1ft) deeper than the base of the root ball. Mix good topsoil (the excavated topsoil where this is of reasonable quality) with peat and sand in the ratio of, parts by volume, five parts soil to two parts peat and one part sand. Add 60g (2oz.) of balanced fertilizer per 300mm³ (1ft³) or per three nine-litre (two-gallon) buckets, mixing all together very thoroughly.

Spray container-grown plants that are in full leaf with an anti-wilting preparation before planting in hot weather.

Planting

Lifted open-ground trees or shrubs which are delivered well in advance of planting must not be allowed to dry out and are best heeled-in until it is possible to plant them. Heeling-in consists of digging a hole of sufficient depth, placing the roots in it and covering them with soil. Any roots which have dried out in transit should be soaked in water for several hours before being set out.

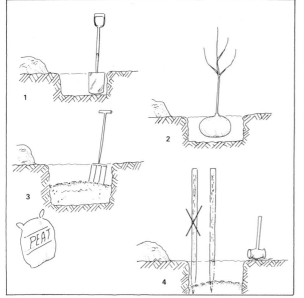

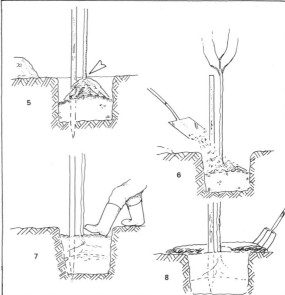

Figure 5a
Planting preparation
1 Dig a hole sufficiently wide and deep to comfortably take each tree
2 Test the hole for size, allowing for filling soil to be placed around the roots
3 Fork in peat or well-rotted compost or manure into the base
4 Position stake correctly where needed and hammer in before planting

Figure 5b
Planting
5 Set trees at the same soil level as before the move
6 Cover the roots with prepared fine compost or peat-enriched good topsoil
7 Firm in the mixture or soil around the roots during the filling process as well as afterwards
8 Place a mulch of well-rotted manure, compost or peat around each tree after planting or in spring

Container-grown plants which cannot be planted at once should be plunged or sunk up to the rim in peat or pulverized bark. Avoid planting when the soil is frozen, baked dry or waterlogged. Ideally, set plants out in warm, moist soil just before or after steady rainfall.

If possible each tree should be positioned for planting so that its stake is on the side of the prevailing wind. Each tree should be planted so that the soil mark is at the same depth as in the nursery before the move. This is most important where trees are budded or grafted near the soil level.

Work the prepared mixture, well moistened, inbetween and around the roots. Joggle the tree up and down as necessary, and firm the mixture around the roots with your heel.

Fasten each tree securely to a support, using a suitable tree tie or twine. If twine is used protect the stem or trunk with a piece of hessian, to prevent damage or abrasion.

When planting on lawns it is wise to leave a 300mm (1ft) wide collar of bare soil around the trunk.

Place a 50mm (1in.) layer of peat, rotted manure or compost around any tree as a mulch.

Tree care programme

Task	To be carried out			
	Spring		*Late*	*spring*
Level vacant land	X	X	X	X
Check/install drainage	X	X	X	X
Apply/spread manure	X	X	X	X
Dig/fork/cultivate vacant ground	X	X	X	X
Spread lime when necessary	X	X	X	X
Final preparation for planting	X	X	X	X
Prepare space for heeling-in	X	X	X	X
Heel-in trees	X	X	X	X
Plant bare root or b-a-w deciduous trees	X	X	—	—
Plant container-grown trees	X	X	X	X
Provide temporary shelter for young trees	X	X	X	X
Lift/plant young trees	X	X	X	—
Water/syringe newly planted trees	—	X	X	X
Apply mulch around trees	X	X	X	X
Surface cultivation	X	X	X	X
Firm newly planted trees after frost/wind	X	X	X	X
Weed	X	X	X	X
Apply top dressing	X	X	X	X
Examine/repair temporary tree shelter	X	X	X	X
Inspect, erect, renew, adjust tree stakes/ties	X	X	X	X
Place tree guards around trunks	X	X	X	X
Dislodge heavy snow resting on trees	X	X	—	—
Prune deciduous trees	X	—	—	—
Root prune excessively vigorous cherries/plums	—	—	—	—
Cut dead/diseased wood out of trees	X	X	X	X
Take cuttings	X	—	—	—
Carry out budding	—	—	—	—
Carry out grafting	—	X	X	—
Layer branches	—	X	X	—

Summer		Late summer		Autumn		Winter	
X	X	X	X	X	X	X	X
X	X	X	X	X	X	X	X
X	X	X	X	X	X	X	X
X	X	X	X	X	X	X	X
X	X	X	X	X	X	X	X
—	X	X	X	X	X	X	X
—	X	X	X	X	X	X	X
—	—	X	X	X	X	X	X
—	—	—	—	—	X	X	X
—	—	X	X	X	X	X	X
—	—	—	X	X	X	X	X
—	—	—	X	X	X	—	—
X	X	X	X	X	—	—	—
X	X	X	—	—	—	—	—
X	X	X	X	X	X	X	X
X	—	—	—	X	X	X	X
X	X	X	X	X	X	X	X
—	—	X	X	X	X	X	X
—	—	—	X	X	X	X	X
X	X	X	X	X	X	X	X
X	X	X	X	X	X	X	X
—	—	—	—	—	X	X	X
—	—	—	X	X	X	X	X
—	—	—	—	X	X	—	—
X	X	X	X	X	X	X	X
X	X	X	X	X	X	X	X
—	X	X	—	—	—	—	—
—	—	—	—	—	—	—	—
—	—	—	X	X	—	—	—

Key
Spring=February/March
Late spring=April/May
Summer=June/July
Late summer=August/September
Autumn=October/November
Winter=December/January

21

Tree care

Following planting the aim of the gardener should be to provide continued good growing conditions and to encourage growth as and where required. This will involve: supplying good root conditions and a satisfactory site environment; handling the trees correctly; and controlling pests, diseases and other problems.

Managing the soil

One of the prime needs of a young tree is to develop and subsequently maintain a strong, healthy root system.

Rainwater should be held by the soil to supply plant needs, and any surplus drained away. In dry spells water young trees before they suffer from drought and cover the soil with a 50mm (2in.) minimum layer of manure, compost or peat, as a mulch to conserve moisture. Also apply a mulch each year in early spring.

To prevent compaction the soil should be loosened occasionally, care being taken not to damage the roots. This stirring enables water and air to reach the lower levels, which ensures that roots can breathe as well as feed.

Firm the ground around young trees loosened by wind or frost.

Weeds should be promptly disposed of to reduce competition for moisture, air and food. Hoe areas of bare earth during the spring and summer months, to control weeds and stir the soil.

During autumn or winter, after planting and subsequently, apply 70–100g per sq. m (2–3oz. per sq. yd) of a general fertilizer, and lightly fork this in.

The feeding of old or neglected trees, which are making little growth, can often induce renewed vigour. The feeding can be done either by top dressing or by spiking.

Top dressing consists of spreading a 50–75mm (2–3in.) layer of soil and manure or peat mixture in the ratio of two parts soil to one part of peat or well rotted material. Sprinkle 100g per sq. in. (3oz. per sq. yd) of general fertilizer over the ground, before applying the top dressing, which should cover the root area under the tree and beyond the drip line – the extremities of the branches.

Spiking, when carefully carried out, can bring about an even more rapid response than top dressing. Make a series of holes 300–450mm (1–1½ft) deep, by 25–50mm (1–2in.) across, spaced 300mm (1ft) apart in the area of the feeding roots near the drip line. Fill the holes with a mixture similar to that suggested above for top dressing, or alternatively use John Innes potting compost No. 2, in either case filling the cavities right to the top.

Top dressing or spiking seems to work very well when carried out during autumn, winter or early spring before the trees break into new season's growth. However, for best results particularly after spiking and top dressing, keep the roots and soil moist, especially during dry weather in spring and summer.

Site improvement

Although there is a limit to the extent to which the environmental conditions of outdoor plants can be controlled, a moderating influence can be exerted.

Slopes which are south-facing and sunny are naturally warmest. However, cold or exposed sites can be improved by screening to give shelter from cold winds. Young trees, and those with tender spring foliage especially, can benefit greatly from the provision of even temporary wattle or hessian screens.

The presence or absence of sun or shade can greatly influence the success or otherwise of trees. Some trees, such as Beech, grow best in dappled shade in the early years, and in full sun when well established. Many Maples and Sorbus require full sun for the strongest colouring effects, but large varieties can become mis-shapen in windswept positions.

Give trees space to grow, and resist the temptation to plant them too close, or at least make sure that you thin out the planting in good time.

Support and protection

One of the obvious needs of young trees is for adequate support until they become established.

Deciduous trees planted small, 600–900mm (2–3ft) high, require nothing more elaborate than a bamboo cane or stick and ties. Bush trees, half-standard and standard forms require more substantial support than whips, as indicated in the pre-planting preparations.

Examine tree stakes and ties regularly and adjust or renew as necessary; stems swaying in the wind can soon be damaged.

Mature or old trees, carrying heavy branches and much foliage, can, when healthy and in good condition, be helped to resist damage from prevailing winds by guying and bracing. This method can also be used to support large newly planted trees. Three or four or more straining wires are evenly spaced around the tree to provide support from wind regardless of direction. Hammer some strong pegs into the ground and attach the tree stem to the pegs with wires. The wires should be covered with rubber tubing or something similar (passing a wire through a length of hose pipe works well) to protect the stem from chafing.

In country districts, especially where rabbits or hares are around, protect young tree stems with plastic guards or fine 12mm (½in.) mesh wire netting.

Pruning and training

This subject can be divided into four categories. The method of pruning depends to a large extent on the age and stage of a tree and its development.

Bush, half-standard and standard trees, which are offered for sale, usually have a basic framework of young branches.

Formation or training pruning consists of building up an initial framework of well spaced branches, by hard cutting and removing unwanted shoots. As most people want quick results and suppliers are anxious to oblige, young trees can usually be obtained with a ready-made initial framework of branches.

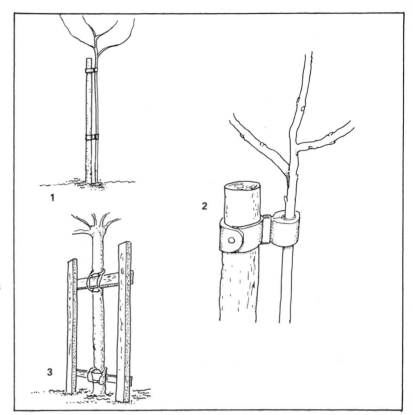

Figure 6
1 Young tree supported by two ties at the top and two-thirds down a single stem
2 Detail showing top tie with the lowest branch and stem clear of the tree stake
3 Heavy trees or those in exposed sites can be tied to cross members, fixed to two stakes, to provide extra support

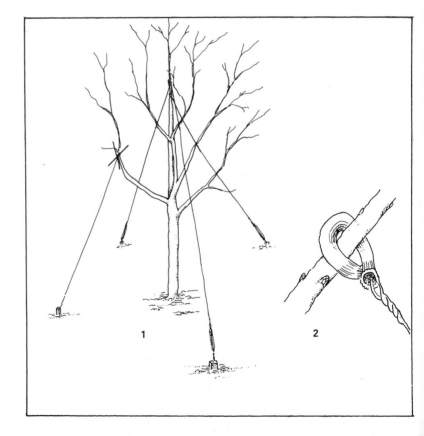

Figure 7
1 Large trees can be held in position by 'guying' in the ground as shown. The stem is attached to pegs, not branches
2 Detail showing wire passed through a length of hosepipe to protect the stem from chafing

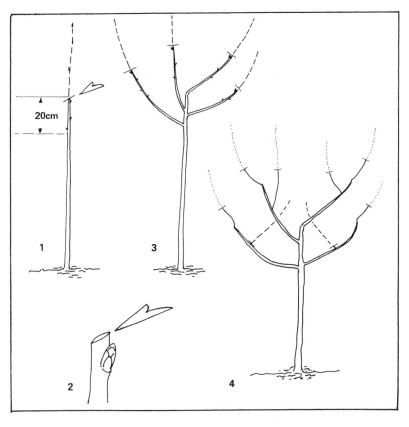

Figure 8
Formation pruning
1 Cut 'whips' about 20cm (8in.) above the point at which the lowest branch is required to emerge from the main stem
2 Detail showing point of cut arrowed about 3mm (⅛in.) above a bud
3 In the second autumn, shorten the shoots by half to two-thirds
4 In the third autumn, remove half to two-thirds of the subsequent shoots and badly-placed growths

Formation pruning

The aim in training young trees is to obtain a strong main stem and good branch framework. In the first autumn cut the tree trunk or stem at about 3mm (⅛in.) above an upward pointing bud and 200–300mm (8–12in.) above the point where you want the lowest main branch to emerge. In the next autumn, cut the subsequent three or four branches back by half to two-thirds, to induce strong growth. If necessary this should be repeated again in the third autumn.

Maintenance pruning

Normal maintenance pruning involves cutting out dead, diseased or crossing branches and removing surplus shoots to thin out and give space for proper development. With most deciduous trees, apart from the occasional thinning, the less pruning the better. However, there are exceptions to every rule. Occasionally among young flowering cherries or plums an odd tree may make much growth but provide little or no blossom; which brings us on to the next item.

Root pruning

This is normally carried out in late summer or autumn, and can be tried as a last resort to induce flowering and fruiting; it often achieves the desired effect. Dig a circular trench, about 600mm (2ft), for young, more for mature trees, from the stem, 300mm (1ft) minimum width and 300–450mm (1–1½ft) deep; and cut the thickest and strongest roots. Return the soil to the trench after pruning.

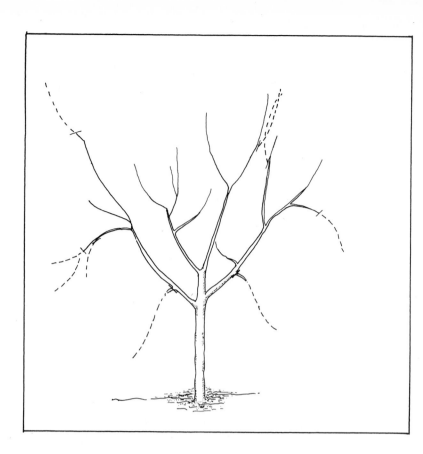

Figure 9
Routine maintenance pruning
consists of cutting out surplus,
crossing or unwanted
downward-growing shoots

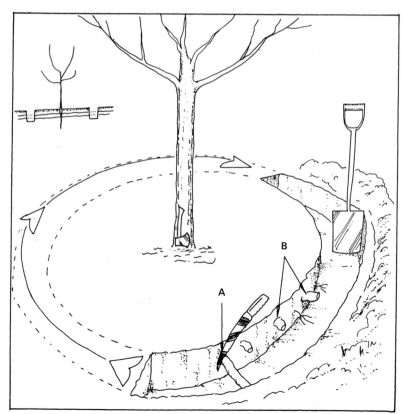

Figure 10
Root pruning, which consists of
severing thick roots about 600mm
(2ft) from the trunk, usually results
in improved flower and fruit
production. Inset shows roots
severed in trenches

Figure 11
Lopping
1 Undercut one-third through the limb, then make the second cut with the saw, arrowed from above
2 Saw off the stump flush with the trunk, again undercutting
3 Smooth off any rough edges with a sharp knife

Remedial pruning
The fourth category consists of what might be termed remedial pruning. Using a saw for tree surgery is sometimes necessary for safety or other reasons, or required to tidy up neglected vegetation. This aspect of pruning is normally best left to qualified operators. However, there are three jobs in this category which can be carried out by the home gardener, always provided the branch size or height involved is manageable. These are listed below.

Lopping branches: this is often necessary where trees have been neglected or are diseased. Cut limbs back to healthy wood, starting at the tips and work inwards, or flush with the main stem. First undercut the bough one-quarter way through close to the main stem, then cut from above, but slightly further in from the trunk. The trunk should not then be damaged by any splitting of heavy branches. The short remaining stub can be sawn off flush with the main stem. Cut or pare off any rough edges with a sharp knife, to leave a smooth finish, and paint over the wound with lead paint or a proprietary sealant.

Crown raising: bush trees can often be improved by the removal of lower branches, which exposes a greater length of stem and leaves more space for access beneath the branches. This process can be repeated over a number of years, gradually increasing the distance between ground level and the lowest branches. Paint over any wounds over 25mm (1in.) in diameter left after pruning.

Crown thinning: as the name suggests, this involves a reduction or cutting out of a proportion of the branches in the head or crown, to

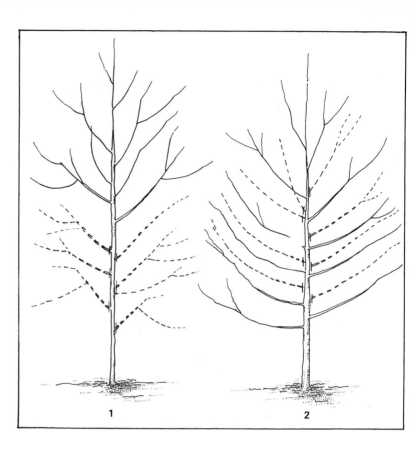

Figure 12
1 Crown raising involves the removal of the lower branches as indicated by the broken lines
2 Crown thinning consists of cutting out surplus boughs, indicated by broken lines, to allow light and air to penetrate among the branches

let in air and daylight. This is occasionally needed, especially with neglected trees. The amount of thinning necessary varies, but the important requirement is that branches should not rub or chafe each other.

Pest and disease control
Fortunately many decorative and ornamental garden trees are not greatly troubled with these problems, but they do arise from time to time. Details of the most commonly encountered pests and diseases are given in the table below.

The principles of successful control rely heavily on preventive measures against pests and diseases. Clean cultivation, removal of dead or diseased tree parts and timely spraying where necessary are all vital. With diseases in particular the application of protective or preventive sprays will not remove the blemishes. The control measures, to be successful, must start long before the symptoms occur. With deciduous trees this ideally means covering the unfolding leaves with a thin film of protective spray and renewing as necessary to maintain a covering film.

Some common pests and diseases, their symptoms and control measures

Problem	Symptoms	Control
Pests		
Aphid, blackfly or greenfly	Colonies of black, blue or green insects on leaves or growing points, causing distortion and leaving a shiny sticky exudate.	Spray with derris, malathion or similar at the first signs. In severe cases on *Malus* or *Prunus* spp. give tar oil winter spray.
Caterpillar	Larvae of various caterpillar-like creatures and holed or eaten leaves.	Spray with derris or fenitrothion when pests appear. In severe outbreaks on *Malus* or *Prunus* give tar oil winter spray.
Leaf miner	Light-coloured lines or blotches on leaves, tunnelled by insects.	Apply diazinon spray.
Scale	Light brown or greyish raised lumps on stems and leaves.	Spray with malathion or petroleum oil.
Woolly aphid	Cotton-wool-like tufts on stems and trunks.	Drench affected areas with dimethoate or malathion.
Diseases		
Honey fungus	Yellow toadstools on dead stumps.	Remove dead stumps. Sterilize soil with formaldehyde six weeks before new planting.
Leaf-spot	Various spotting of leaves.	Spray with copper or similar fungicide.
Mildews	Powdery or downy whitish covering on leaves.	Spray with benomyl.
Peach leaf curl	Reddish or dark distorted peach leaves.	Apply benomyl or copper sprays.
Rust	Brown or yellowish dust on leaves.	Spray with thiram.
Scab	Dark spots on fruits and leaves of Malus or Cotoneaster.	Apply benomyl or copper sprays.
Silver leaf	Silvering of leaves on Cherry or Plum.	Remove and burn affected branches.
Tar spot	Sooty blotches on leaves of Sycamore and Maple.	Spray with copper fungicide.

Sprays should not be made up indoors and should be thoroughly mixed before use.

Spraying or dusting should not be carried out in wet, freezing or windy conditions.

Tar oil should only be used after leaf fall and before early spring. It is most important that the buds should be dormant.

Propagation

Trees can be increased in various ways, but propagating is not for the impatient 'instant' gardener, rather for the nurseryman, dedicated enthusiast or the conservationist. The two fundamental ways of increasing trees are: from seeds; or by vegetative means.

Raising from seeds

This method has advantages and disadvantages.

When trees are raised from seed they often differ from the parent plant, and can occasionally give rise to a new variety. However, the chances of producing a garden-worthy variety are slender unless large numbers of seedlings are involved.

Seeds provide a means of large-scale increase of a species, but named varieties do not always come true to type and have to be increased from cuttings, layers or grafting.

Breaking dormancy

Some tree seeds, such as Birch, can be sown fresh.

Other seeds, among them Sorbus and Thorn need preparing before sowing to break the dormancy.

One preparatory process, known as stratification, consists of subjecting the seeds to the action of frost for one or possibly two winters before sowing. To stratify small quantities, mix the seeds with two or three times their volume of sand. Place the mixture in a square of muslin, the corners of which are gathered together, tied and labelled. The muslin bags are then buried 50–75mm (2–3in.) deep in sand and covered with fine mesh wire netting to keep mice and birds out. The seeds are buried outside in autumn and are lifted, cleaned and sown in early-mid spring. Soaking seeds in warm water, for six to eight hours before sowing, can assist rapid germination.

Sowing seed

Sow seeds thinly in 125mm (5in.) pots of John Innes seed compost, with a thin layer of gravel chippings placed in the bottom for drainage. Cover the seeds with a layer of fine compost or coarse sand, to double their diameter in depth. Place a sheet of glass or plastic and a sheet of paper over the pots. Put in a cool greenhouse or frame to germinate. Prick the seedlings out when large enough to handle, harden off and plant out hardy kinds in a sheltered corner.

Vegetative propagation

Named varieties or those possessing some unique characteristic have to be raised by vegetative means. Cuttings, suckers and layers are the usual methods for amateurs, with budding and grafting being left to professionals.

Half-ripe cuttings

This method involves detaching from the parent plant, in summer, young, firm, healthy shoots of the current season's growth, 75–100mm (3–4in.) long, not bearing flowers. Using a very sharp knife carefully cut the shoot just below a leaf joint and gently remove the lower leaf or two. Dip the cut end into hormone rooting powder and insert the prepared cutting to a depth of half its length in sandy soil in a clean frame. The cuttings should be shaded from strong sunlight until they are rooted. This method has proved very successful under controlled conditions.

Hardwood cuttings

In autumn, firm, current season's growths, 150–250mm (6–10in.) long are cut below a leaf joint, or taken with a heel – a piece of older wood attached to the bottom of the shoot. These cuttings can then be inserted to half their length in sandy soil in frames to overwinter.

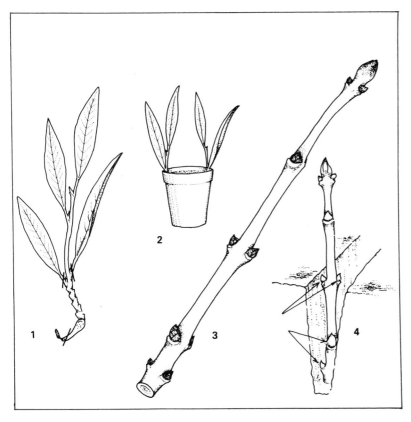

Figure 13
1 A half-ripe (semi-hardwood) Willow cutting before trimming off lower leaves and 'tail' as indicated by short lines
2 Insert prepared half-ripe cuttings around the edge of a pot, containing suitable cutting compost
3 Prepared hardwood cutting of Poplar
4 Place hardwood cutting in shallow trench and firm the soil around the base. The buds arrowed should be removed to prevent suckering

In spring, suitably hardened-off rooted cuttings can be planted out in nursery beds to grow on.

Layering
This operation is usually carried out in spring or autumn as follows.

Select a pencil-thick young stem within easy reach of the ground. Make a slanting cut halfway through the shoot about 200–250mm (8–10in.) from the tip.

Scoop out a shallow hole about 50–75mm (2–3in.) deep. Then place the cut portion of the stem into the cavity and secure it with a peg to hold down the branch firmly. Bend the end of the shoot up vertically

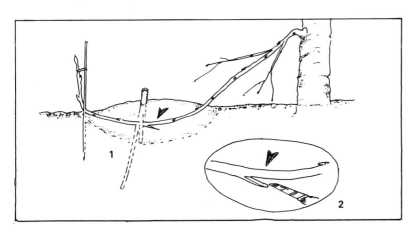

Figure 14
1 Layering, showing a 'pencil-thick' shoot pegged down in the hollow, with the tip tied vertically
2 Inset, showing detail of slanting cut

and tie the tip to a stick so that it points upwards.

Cover the cut portion and fill the cavity with clean sandy compost. Keep this well watered in dry weather. When the layer is growing, 12 or 24 months after layering, sever it from the parent tree, then plant it out.

Stooling and air-layering are more suitable for nurserymen.

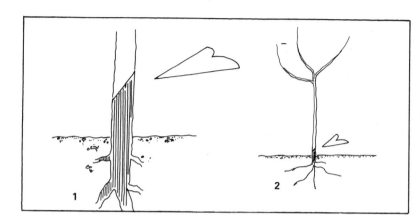

Figure 15
1 Detail of graft union of rootstock, shaded, with scion, or desired variety in white
2 Grafted tree showing rootstock and scion, with the point of the graft union arrowed

Budding and grafting

Budding and grafting are more in the province of the professional. However, it is useful to understand the rudiments of budding and grafting when purchasing trees.

Some trees grow better when they are budded or grafted on the roots of a closely related tree. The flowering, foliage or fruiting variety takes the place of the top of the rootstock. This is often done with Cherries, for example. Some rootstocks are highly resistant to bacteria canker. Where a susceptible, but desirable variety is budded on disease-resistant stock, some measure of protection for the required variety is given.

The trees

Choosing a tree

Before going into the detailed descriptions of each tree, readers may like to consult the following lists, which have been compiled for quick and easy reference.

Fastigiate forms
Betula pendula 'Fastigiata'
Carpinus betulus 'Columnaris'
Fagus sylvatica 'Fastigiata'
Sorbus aucuparia 'Fastigiata'
Sorbus hybrida 'Fastigiata'

Pyramidal types
Liquidambar styraciflua and
  varieties
Malus tschonoskii
Salix matsudana

Weeping or pendulous trees
Betula pendula 'Dalecarlica'
Betula pendula 'Tristis'
Betula pendula 'Youngii'
Carpinus betulus 'Pendula'
Fagus sylvatica 'Aurea Pendula'
Fagus sylvatica 'Pendula'
Fagus sylvatica 'Purpurea Pendula'
Fraxinus excelsior 'Aurea Pendula'
Fraxinus excelsior 'Pendula'
Laburnum anagyroides 'Pendulum'
Parrotia persica 'Pendula'
Prunus avium 'Pendula'
Prunus cerasifera 'Pendula'
Prunus persica 'Albo plena
  Pendula'
Prunus persica 'Windle Weeping'
Prunus subhirtella 'Pendula Plena
  Rosea'
Prunus subhirtella 'Pendula Rosea'
Prunus subhirtella 'Pendula Rubra'
Pyrus salicifolia 'Pendula'
Salix matsudana 'Pendula'
Sorbus aria 'Pendula'
Sorbus aucuparia 'Pendula'

Upright or columnar habit
Betula pendula
Carpinus betulus
Carpinus betulus 'Incisa'
Carpinus betulus 'Purpurea'
Cercidiphyllum japonicum
Cotoneaster frigidus
Cotoneaster frigidus 'Fructuluteo'
Eucalyptus gunnii

Laburnum anagyroides and
  varieties
Liriodendron tulipifera
Liriodendron tulipifera
  'Fastigiatum'
Populus alba
Robinia pseudoacacia 'Pyramidalis'
Sorbus aria
Sorbus aria 'Lutescens'
Sorbus aria 'Pendula'
Sorbus x hybrida

*Globose, rounded or spreading
forms*
Acer campestre
Acer griseum
Acer japonicum and varieties
Acer negundo and varieties
Acer pensylvanicum and varieties
Acer platanoides and varieties
Acer pseudoplatanus and varieties
Aesculus x carnea and varieties
Catalpa bignonioides
Catalpa bignonioides 'Aurea'
Ceris siliquastrum and varieties
Crataegus crus-galli and varieties
Crataegus oxyacantha and varieties
Davidia involucrata
Davidia involucrata vilmoriniana
Fagus sylvatica
Fagus sylvatica 'Purpurea'
Fagus sylvatica 'Zlatia'
Fraxinus excelsior
Gleditsia triacanthos and varieties
Malus hupehensis and varieties
Malus purpurea
Morus nigra
Parrotia persica
Paulownia fargesii
Paulownia tomentosa
Prunus avium
Prunus avium 'Plena'
Prunus cerasifera and varieties
Prunus dulcis
Prunus dulcis 'Alba'
Prunus dulcis 'Praecox'
Prunus dulcis 'Roseoplena'

Prunus padus and varieties
Prunus persica and varieties
Prunus serrulata and varieties
Prunus subhirtella and varieties
Ptelea trifoliata
Quercus coccinea 'Splendens'
Quercus ilex
Quercus rubra
Robinia pseudoacacia
Robinia pseudoacacia 'Frisia'
Robinia pseudoacacia 'Inermis'
Sorbus aucuparia
Sorbus aucuparia 'Asplenifolia'
Sorbus aucuparia 'Xanthocarpa'
Tilia platyphyllos 'Rubra'

Trees with autumn colour
Acer campestre
Acer japonicum
Acer pensylvanicum
Acer platanoides
Acer pseudoplatanus
Aesculus x carnea
Betula pendula
Carpinus betulus
Catalpa bignonioides
Cercidiphyllum japonicum
Cercis siliqiastrum
Cotoneaster frigidus
Crataegus crus-galli
Crataegus oxyacantha
Fagus sylvatica
Fraxinus excelsior
Gleditsia triacanthos
Koelreuteria paniculata
Liquidambar styraciflua
Liriodendron tulipifera
Malus hupehensis
Malus x purpurea
Malus tschonoskii
Parrotia persica
Paulownia tomentosa
Populus alba
Prunus avium
Prunus serrulata
Quercus coccinea
Quercus rubra
Robinia pseudoacacia

Salix matsudana
Sorbus aria
Sorbus aucuparia
Sorbus x hybrida
Tilia platyphyllos
    The majority of the varieties of these species are also noteworthy for the provision of autumn colour and interest.

Trees with colourful autumn berries or fruits
Cotoneaster frigidus
Crataegus crus-galli
Crataegus oxyacantha
Koelreuteria paniculata
Malus hupehensis
Malus x purpurea
Malus tschonoskii
Sorbus aria
Sorbus aucuparia
Sorbus x hybrida

Trees noted for trunk, stem and bud, providing interest in winter
Acer griseum
Acer pensylvanicum
Acer pseudoplatanus
Aesculus x carnea
Betula pendula
Carpinus betulus
Cercidiphyllum japonicum
Crataegus oxyacantha
Eucalyptus gunnii
Fagus sylvatica
Fraxinus excelsior
Parrotia persica
Prunus serrulata
Prunus subhirtella
Robinia pseudoacacia
Salix matsudana
Tilia platyphyllos

Trees for acid soils
Acer japonicum
Acer pensylvanicum
Acer platanoides
Acer pseudoplatanus
Aesculus x carnea
Betula pendula
Crataegus crus-galli
Crataegus oxyacantha
Laburnum anagyriodes
Liquidambar styraciflua
Liriodendron tulipifera
Malus x purpurea
Malus tschonoskii
Parrotia persica
Prunus padus
Prunus persica and varieties
Prunus serrulata
Quercus coccinea
Quercus rubra

Robinia pseudoacacia
Sorbus aria
Sorbus aucuparia
    The varieties of these species can also be grown on acid soils.

Trees for alkaline or chalk soils
Acer campestre
Acer negundo
Acer platanoides
Acer pseudoplatanus
Aesculus x carnea
Carpinus betulus
Cercidiphyllum japonicum
Cercis siliquastrum
Cotoneaster frigidus
Crataegus crus-galli
Crataegus oxyacantha
Fagus sylvatica
Fraxinus excelsior
Gleditsia triacanthos
Populus alba
Prunus avium
Prunus cerasifera
Prunus dulcis
Prunus subhirtella
Pyrus salicifolia
Quercus ilex
Robinia pseudoacacia
Salix matsudana
Sorbus aria
Sorbus x hybrida
Tilia platyphyllos
    Varieties of these species are also generally suitable.

Trees for coastal districts
Acer campestre
Acer platanoides
Acer pseudoplatanus
Aesculus x carnea
Betula pendula
Carpinus betulus
Cercis siliquastrum
Cotoneaster frigidus
Crataegus crus-galli
Crataegus oxyacantha
Eucalyptus gunnii
Fagus sylvatica
Fraxinus excelsior
Laburnum anagyroides
Malus hupehensis
Malus tschonoskii
Parrotia persica
Populus alba
Prunus avium
Prunus cerasifera
Prunus dulcis
Prunus padus
Prunus persica
Prunus serrulata
Prunus subhirtella
Pyrus salicifolia

Quercus ilex
Robinia pseudoacacia
Sorbus aria
Sorbus aucuparia
Sorbus x hybrida
    Varieties of these species are also suitable.

Trees for town planting
Acer japonicum
Acer negundo
Acer platanoides
Acer pseudoplatanus
Aesculus x carnea
Betula pendula
Carpinus betulus
Cotoneaster frigidus
Crataegus crus-galli
Crataegus oxyacantha
Fagus sylvatica
Fraxinus excelsior
Laburnum anagyroides
Malus hupehensis
Malus x purpurea
Malus tschonoskii
Morus nigra
Prunus avium
Prunus cerasifera
Prunus dulcis
Prunus padus
Prunus persica
Prunus serrulata
Prunus subhirtella
Robinia pseudoacacia
Salix matsudana
Sorbus aria
Sorbus aucuparia
Sorbus x hybrida
Tilia platyphyllos
    Varieties of these species can also be used.

Trees suitable for shade
Acer griseum
Acer negundo variegatum
Acer japonicum
Acer japonicum 'Aconitifolium'
Acer japonicum 'Vitifolium'
Acer pensylvanicum
Acer platanoides and varieties
Acer pseudoplatanus and varieties
Betula pendula and varieties
Carpinus betulus and varieties
Cotoneaster frigidus
Cotoneaster frigidus 'Fructuluteo'
Crataegus oxyacantha
Fagus sylvatica and varieties
Laburnum anagyroides and
    varieties
Liquidambar styraciflua when
    young
Liriodendron tulipifera when young
Prunus avium

Prunus cerasifera
Prunus padus
Prunus serrulata
Quercus ilex
Robinia pseudoacacia
Salix matsudana

While many trees can tolerate partial shade for part of the day, overcrowding or overhanging branches are usually harmful. Flowering trees or those noted for autumn colour of leaves and fruits are generally more effective in full sun.

Trees for dry soils
Acer campestre
Acer platanoides and varieties
Acer pseudoplatanus and varieties
Betula pendula
Cercis siliquastrum and varieties
Crataegus oxyacantha and varieties
Eucalyptus gunnii
Fagus sylvatica
Laburnum anagyroides
Populus alba
Pyrus salicifolia 'Pendula'
Robinia pseudoacacia

Robinia pseudoacacia 'Inermis'
Sorbus aria
Sorbus aucuparia
Sorbus x hybrida
Sorbus x hybrida 'Fastigiata'

Trees, which are grown on dry land usually have certain fairly well defined characteristics when compared with plants grown on wet soils. Flowering is more prolific, though of shorter duration. The colouring of flowers, fruits and leaves is more vivid and earlier. The rate of tree growth and increase in size is slower.

Trees for wet conditions
Acer platanoides
Acer pseudoplatanus and varieties
Betula pendula and varieties
Carpinus betulus and varieties
Crataegus oxyacantha and varieties
Fraxinus excelsior and varieties
Laburnum anagyroides and
  varieties
Populus alba
Prunus avium and varieties
Prunus cerasifera and varieties

Prunus padus and varieties
Prunus serrulata
Salix matsudana and varieties
Sorbus aria
Sorbus aucuparia and varieties
Sorbus x hybrida
Tilia platyphyllos and varieties

Trees for the coldest sites
Acer platanoides
Acer pseudoplatanus
Betula pendula
Carpinus betulus
Crataegus crus-galli
Crataegus oxyacantha
Fagus sylvatica
Fraxinus excelsior
Laburnum anagyroides
Malus hupehensis
Malus tschonoskii
Prunus avium
Prunus cerasifera
Pyrus salicifolia
Quercus rubra
Sorbus aria
Sorbus aucuparia
Sorbus hybrida

Explanatory notes to individual descriptions of trees

The information about each tree is necessarily brief and some qualifications of the comments are essential to enable the reader to grasp the facts more readily.

Names   The botanical name currently in use is given first, followed by the natural order or group to which the plant belongs, e.g. *Acer campestre* (Nat order) Aceraceae.

The English or American popular name appears below.

Varieties are referred to elsewhere.

Uses   Due to differences of size, habit or colour most trees are better suited to some purposes than others. The comments which follow refer to the species or type unless indicated otherwise.

Description   The appearance, dimensions, growth rate and life span are influenced greatly by local conditions of climate, site, soil and method of cultivation. The facts and figures given are approximate and represent average characteristics likely to be encountered under normal garden conditions. However, considerable variation can and does occur even within quite short distances.

Hardiness   in plants is the ability to survive without special protection in normal conditions. This quality is greatly influenced by climate, and by local factors such as altitude, aspect, exposure and cultivation. The trees have been classified according to hardiness, among other qualities, into three main categories, A,B, and C and which relate to the climatic zones on the maps on page 13. Plants which are borderline, are indicated by two letters, e.g. A/B or B/C.

In any broad climatic zone, there are inevitably sites which are particularly favourable or otherwise. Locations that are at high altitudes, or are exposed or north-facing in, say, climatic zone B, might provide conditions equivalent to zone A. The converse is also applicable.

For our purposes here, trees in category:

A can be grown in a cool temperate zone

B can be grown in a mild temperate zone

C can be grown in a warm temperate zone

An indication of the growth rate normally met with is shown in the summary chart on pages 138-141.

Features   The comments on the main qualities which make a tree attractive relate to the species or type unless indicated otherwise.

Pollution   In towns and cities, fumes and gases in the air, soot, oil or other deposits are a normal hazard to plants. Those trees which can grow, flower and flourish in spite of these difficulties are indicated as being tolerant, resistant or otherwise.

Non-poisonous   trees are those which normally present no danger to people or pets.

Varieties   When choosing trees for a particular purpose or characteristic, often a variety is more suitable than the species from which it originated. While a tree type, for example, may be suitable for large spaces, narrow upright selections or varieties appropriate for confined areas, may be available, such as the fastigiate form of Hornbeam.

Requirements The growth and development of garden trees depends largely on how well their needs are satisfied with regard to climate, site, soil and other conditions. Where conditions are less than perfect, growth and development will also fall short of the best results possible.

An indication of the ideal conditions which are often difficult to provide is given together with the degree of latitude that is possible, and still ensure satisfactory results. Seasonal and weather variations can upset the best calculations, even when other requirements are met.

Notes on culture

Planting Generally small trees can be transplanted and become established more readily in new surroundings than large specimens, often quickly catching up and overtaking the latter. The season of planting and suggested size refer to lifted open-ground trees except where stated to the contrary.

Space The area or distance indicated is the space needed by average trees at maturity.

Pruning The requirements here vary according to the size and stage of development of individual trees.

Underplanting can only be practised where there is sufficient head-room, and applies mainly to half-standard and standard forms of trees.

Pest and disease control These notes should be read in conjunction with the table on page 29.

Propagation The methods indicated are those more usually adopted. Most people prefer to buy rather than raise young trees, for propagation is a time consuming exercise. An understanding of how trees are raised can be helpful in their planting and aftercare. Grafted trees should not be deeply planted to avoid scion-rooting for example.

Season of interest table This is designed to indicate the main features and the approximate time they can be seen and enjoyed. The feature items are self-explanatory. Fruit also covers items such as berries and nuts. Where an entry is omitted, the feature concerned is either insignificant or lacking.

Growth rate and qualities table The dimensions given are examples of the average rate of growth which can be expected under normal garden conditions. Differences in planting size will be reflected in the height and width at five and at twenty years afterwards.

The root spread at planting time will usually approximate the width in the case of open-ground trees. The spread of roots with container-grown plants can vary from one- to two-thirds the width above ground.

Hardiness. This follows the system indicated elsewhere, namely A=cool temperate, B=mild temperate and C=warm temperate.

Wind-firm 1=very secure rooting 2=wind-firm 3=moderately wind-firm, which may need staking for many years in exposed sites.

Plant care profile Minimum, average and high refer to the degree of attention that is normally needed to keep trees healthy, tidy and in good condition.

Maintenance covers such aspects as pest and disease control, leaf clearance, feeding and other cultural requirements.

Acer campestre – ACERACEAE
Common Maple, Field Maple, Hedge Maple

Origin   Europe (including Britain).
A hardy deciduous tree or shrub.

Uses
Hedge Maples are primarily
amenity trees providing height,
shelter and privacy. They may be
used to form a windbreak or
planted as single specimens on
lawns or in shubberies, or in groups
of two or three where space
permits. They are also used in open
spaces and residential areas in
lowland rural and town situations.

Description
Dimensions   Average ultimate size
4–6m (13–20ft) high by 3m (10ft)
wide, but old specimens double that
size have been noted.
Rate of growth   Usually slow, but
sometimes moderate in young trees.
Life span   Under good conditions
trees of 200 or more years old can
be expected.
Habit   A neat, round-headed tree.
Leaves   Three- or five-lobed
reddish-pink leaves in spring,
turning green and then to pink and
yellow shades in autumn.
Flowers   Sparce, greenish and
visually insignificant.
Fruits   In autumn mature trees
carry attractive winged seeds, green
at first, later turning colour like the
leaves.
Bark   Greyish-brown, often
concealed by foliage.

Features
In central, southern and eastern
England this Maple often occurs in
hedgerows, hence its name. The
Hedge Maple is wind-firm and will
stand cutting back. It does not have
poisonous fruits or foliage, nor are
the seeds a nuisance as those of
Sycamore often are. The neat habit,
and restful foliage are endearing
qualities.
Pollution   Tolerates average town
conditions.
Non-poisonous.

Varieties
Acer campestre 'Pulverulentum'.
Leaves speckled with white dots
and markings.
Acer campestre 'Schwerinii'.
Leaves opening purple, but turn
green in summer.

Requirements
Position   Sheltered lowland areas
in the mild temperate zone suit this
tree. In harsh climates or on
exposed sites it is inclined to be
little more than a shrub. It will
tolerate light shade, but sunny sites
produce the best colouring effects.
Soil   Well drained neutral or
chalky loams with a pH range of
6.5–7.5 are suitable.

Notes on culture
Planting   Trees up to 2.5m (8ft)
high should be planted from
autumn to spring. Stake and tie all
trees after planting.
Space   Allow single specimen trees
a minimum area of 3m (10ft)
diameter and half the same distance
again from buildings.
Pruning   This consists chiefly of
pruning to form the initial
framework of branches. Subsequent
requirements are minimal.
Underplanting   Established trees
may be underplanted with low
ground-cover plants and/or bulbs.
Pest and disease control   Not
usually necessary. Caterpillars may
be checked by spraying with derris
or fenitrothion, mildew and tar spot
by benomyl and copper fungicide
sprays respectively.

Propagation By seeds sown in autumn. Named varieties by grafting in spring; budding in summer; or layering in autumn.

Season of interest	Winter	Spring	Late spring	Summer	Late summer	Autumn
In full leaf			X———————————	—————	—————————	X
Autumn colour						X—X
Flowers						
Fruits					X—X	
Bark and stem						

The following five characteristics determine to a great extent the amount of attention a specific tree requires.

	When planted	5 years	20 years
Height	1·8 m	2·5 m	3·6 m
Width	1·0 m	2·0 m	3·0 m
Root spread		3·0 m	4·0 m
Hardiness	B/C	B	B
Wind-firm		2	1

Plant care profile

	Minimum	Average	High
Site needs		X	
Soil needs		X	
Pruning	X———X		
Staking	X———X		
Maintenance	X———X		

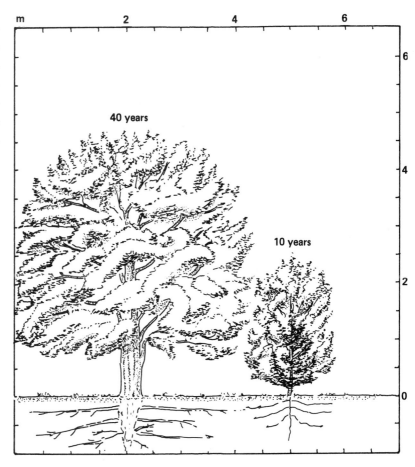

40 years

10 years

Acer griseum – ACERACEAE
Paperbark Maple

Origin China.
A hardy deciduous tree.

Uses
If the Paperbark Maple is planted on a lawn as a specimen tree the autumn leaf colouring and year-round attraction of the trunk will be seen to advantage.

Description
Dimensions Average ultimate size 3–5m (10–17ft) high by 1.8–2.5m (6–8ft) wide. However, under good conditions trees can grow to double this height and half as wide again.
Rate of growth Slow.
Life span Cannot be estimated with certainty, but present indications are that trees over 50 years old will last a good few years yet.
Habit A beautiful, small, round-headed tree.
Leaves Typically three-lobed. The autumn colourings of the leaves, which turn to red, crimson and orange shades, are outstanding.
Flowers Provide little colour and often sparce.
Fruits Brownish winged nutlets, when mature.
Bark The Paperbark Maple owes its name to its papery, peeling bark, which reveals a pleasing orange-buff underlayer.

Features
The chief attractions are: the autumn colouring of the leaves and; the unusual peeling bark with the orange-buff underlayer.
When established this Maple is firmly anchored by the roots. It does not appear to have any bad habits.
Pollution Tolerates average town conditions.
Non-poisonous.

Varieties
There are no other readily available varieties of this tree, which deserves to be better known.

Requirements
Position The best trees are found in lowland areas in the mild or-warm temperate zones. However, other Maples grow well in sheltered lowland sites in slightly colder areas, and the Paperbark Maple might be worth trying. The best autumn colourings are obtained from trees grown in sheltered, sunny situations, but this Maple will tolerate light shade.
Soil Well drained slightly acid or neutral medium loams, with a pH of 6.5–7, have given good results. Shallow, gravelly land and heavy clay soils need to be improved before planting.

Notes on culture
Planting Small trees, up to 2m (7ft), should be planted between autumn and spring. Stake and tie immediately after planting.
Space Give this Maple an area of 2.5m (8ft) diameter for development and half the same distance again from buildings.
Pruning Prune to form the initial framework of branches. Subsequent requirements are minimal.
Underplanting Once the Paperbark Maple has developed a good crown and is root-firm it may be underplanted with ground-cover plants or bulbs. Shrubs would conceal part of the bark.
Pest and disease control If necessary caterpillars may be checked with a derris or fenitrothion spray, leaf-spot and

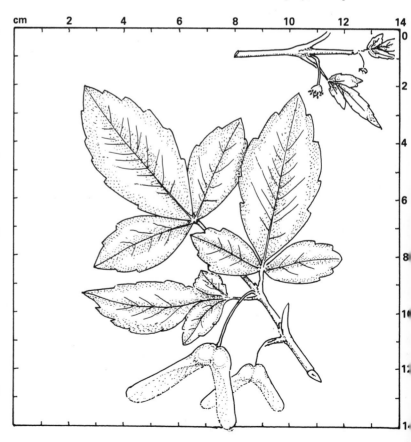

fungus diseases with a copper fungicide. Trees in light shade may develop a green algal covering of trunk and branches, spoiling the effect of the orange underbark. An annual winter wash of tar oil will check this nuisance. Protect any delicate plants beneath with plastic sheeting when spraying is carried out.

Propagation By seeds sown in spring; or layering in autumn.

Season of interest	Winter	Spring	Late spring	Summer	Late summer	Autumn
In full leaf			X———		—X	
Autumn colour					X———	—X
Flowers						
Fruits						
Bark and stem	X———					—X

The following five characteristics determine to a great extent the amount of attention a specific tree requires.

	When planted	5 years	20 years
Height	1·5 m	2·4 m	4·0 m
Width	750 mm	1·5 m	3·0 m
Root spread		2·5 m	4·0 m
Hardiness	C	B/C	B/C
Wind-firm		2/3	2

Plant care profile

	Minimum Average High
Site needs	X———X
Soil needs	X
Pruning	X———X
Staking	X———X
Maintenance	X

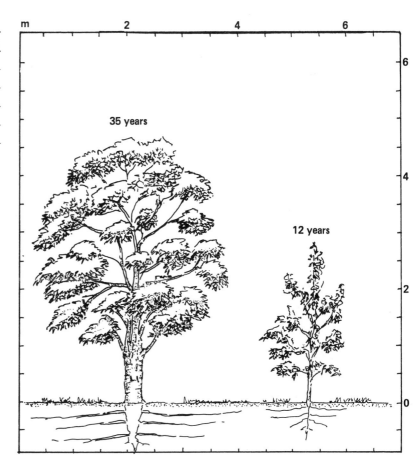

35 years

12 years

41

Acer japonicum – ACERACEAE
Japanese Maple, Full-moon Maple

Origin　Japan.
A moderately hardy deciduous tree.

Uses

These ornamental Maples are best planted singly as specimen trees or in small groups. They can be seen to advantage on lawns or among low ground-cover plants.

Description

Dimensions　Average ultimate size around 4.5–6m (15–20ft) high by 2–3m (7–10ft) wide. Occasionally well grown old specimens in favourable situations can attain double that size.
Rate of growth　Variable, moderate in the early stages, decreasing with age.
Life span　Trees live for upwards of 50 years in congenial surroundings.
Habit　Bushy.
Leaves　Attractive seven- to eleven-fingered leaves, which turn to crimson shades in autumn. The many-fingered leaves help to distinguish this species from other Maples.
Flowers　Colourless in comparison with the leaves.
Fruits　The brownish winged nutlets add little to the effect of the foliage.
Bark　Dull grey-brown, often concealed during the summer months, by leaves.

Features

Leaf shape, but most outstanding are summer and autumn foliage colours of the foliage. The young leaves are rather sensitive to spring frosts and cold winds; wind-firm.
Pollution　Moderately tolerant, young emerging leaves less resistant to fumes than fully expanded growth.
Non-poisōnous.

Varieties

Acer japonicum 'Aconitifolium'. Leaves deeply lobed, turning crimson in autumn.
Acer japonicum 'Aureum'. Slower-growing, and tending to make a smaller tree. Attractive pale yellow leaves that persist through summer and turn to crimson shades in autumn.
Acer japonicum 'Vitifolium'. Leaves broad, vine-shaped, turning to brilliant shades of crimson in autumn.

Requirements

Position　This tree will grow well in the warm temperate zone if it is given a sheltered position, protected from cold winds but preferably in full sun for the best colour effects. South- and west-facing aspects are best. It can be successfully grown in coastal districts, provided protection from sea spray is given. Japanese Maples are sensitive to late spring frosts and to cold winds, both of which can cause leaf-scorch. This condition is often more unsightly than serious, however, with trees growing away again as weather conditions improve.
Soil　Well drained loams, acid or slightly acid, pH 5.5–6.5, and with abundant supplies of organic matter are preferred.

Notes on culture

Planting When selecting a tree choose a well rooted one with a bushy crown of good shape. Plant small trees, up to 2m (7ft) high, in autumn. Stake and tie all trees at planting time, and keep them supported until established.

Space Allow individual trees an area of 3m (10ft) minimum diameter and a similar distance from buildings, avoiding exposed positions.

Pruning Trim young trees to form a balanced framework of branches. In later years prune to shape only.

Underplanting Established trees may be underplanted with low ground-cover plants. Plants requiring acid soil conditions, such as heathers, azaleas and rhododendrons, grow well and look attractive in association with *A. japonicum.*

Pest and disease control Apply insecticide and fungicide sprays against leaf-eating pests and mildew if these appear.

Propagation By seeds sown in autumn. Named varieties by grafting in spring; or layering in autumn.

Season of interest	Winter	Spring	Late spring	Summer	Late summer	Autumn
In full leaf			X———	———	———X	
Autumn colour					X——	—→X
Flowers						
Fruits						
Bark and stem						

The following five characteristics determine to a great extent the amount of attention a specific tree requires.

	When planted	5 years	20 years
Height	1·2 m	2·1 m	3·5 m
Width	750 mm	1·5 m	2·5 m
Root spread		2·0 m	3·5 m
Hardiness	C	C	C
Wind-firm		2	1/2

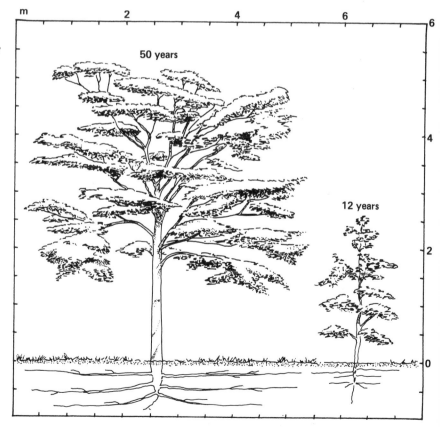

Plant care profile

	Minimum	Average	High
Site needs		X———X	
Soil needs		X———X	
Pruning	X———X		
Staking	X———X		
Maintenance		X———X	

Acer negundo – ACERACEAE
Box Elder

Origin North America.
A moderately hardy deciduous tree.

Uses
These trees may be planted as specimens in lawns or as general planting among shrubs.
Plants grown in tubs can be used in restricted spaces or roof gardens.

Description
Dimensions Average ultimate size 6–7.5m (20–25ft) high by 3–4m (10–13ft) wide. Well grown mature trees in warm temperate conditions have exceeded these dimensions.
Rate of growth Fairly rapid in the early years, decreasing to moderate.
Life span Usually longer than that of many Japanese Maples.
Habit Variable. In dry, sunny situations the crown can be quite dense and compact. In shaded, cooler and wetter conditions the branches are more open.
Leaves Green, three- or five-lobed, but lack autumn colour change, occasionally yellowing.
Flowers Male and female occur on different trees, but are not colourful.
Fruits Brownish winged nutlets.
Bark Dull greyish-brown, often concealed by foliage.

Features
Makes a handsome specimen tree in grass or lawn where subdued or quiet effects are required. Normally wind-firm. Variegated forms are more colourful, but occasionally produce the odd green shoot reverting back to type, but otherwise these trees present few problems.
Pollution Usually satisfactory in towns.
Non-poisonous.

Varieties
Acer negundo 'Auratum' (syn. 'Aureum'). Slower growing than the type. Yellow leaves.
Acer negundo californicum Quick growing, produces rather pleasing pink-winged seeds.
Acer negundo 'Elegans' (syn. 'Elegantissimum'). Leaves marked with yellow.
Acer negundo 'Variegatum'. White variegated leaves.

Requirements
Position Sheltered but sunny situations in most lowland parts of the mild temperate zone, including coastal areas, suit this tree. Confine planting to milder districts.

Soil *A. negundo* and varieties will grow quite happily in various soil types, so long as the soil is deep, well drained and of a loam nature. Near-neutral soils, pH 6.5–7, suit best, but they will tolerate a wider range, 5.7–7.5.

Notes on culture
Planting Trees up to 2.5m (8ft) high should be planted between autumn and spring. Stake and tie trees at planting.
Space Allow these trees 3–4m (10–13ft) diameter space, except where two or three are planted in a group, when 2–2.5m (7–8ft) between trees in the group is possible. Avoid planting closer to buildings than 3m (10ft).

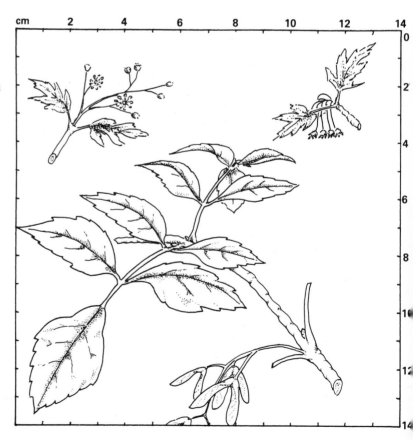

Pruning Prune to form branch framework in young specimens. Thereafter it is necessary to trim only to keep in shape or to remove reverted growths – green-leaved shoots among variegated, for example.

Underplanting The roots of Box Elder are not too exhausting, so some underplanting with shrubs or other plants is possible. These trees associate well with a wide range of chalk-loving plants, flowering shrubs and bulbs.

Pest and disease control This is rarely needed, but when planting after other Maples fill the tree pits with fresh prepared soil. This lessens the chances of infection by root or crown canker.

Propagation By seeds sown in autumn. Named varieties by grafting in spring or layering in autumn.

Season of interest	Winter	Spring	Late spring	Summer	Late summer	Autumn
In full leaf			X———————————			—X
Autumn colour						
Flowers						
Fruits						
Bark and stem						

The following five characteristics determine to a great extent the amount of attention a specific tree requires.

	When planted	5 years	20 years
Height	1·8 m	3·0 m	4·5 m
Width	750 mm	2·0 m	4·0 m
Root spread		3·0 m	5·0 m
Hardiness	B/C	B	B
Wind-firm		2	1

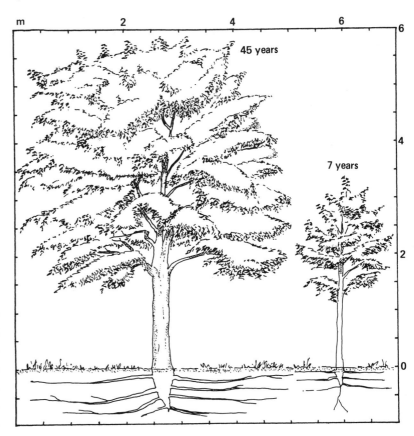

Plant care profile

	Minimum	Average	High
Site needs		X	
Soil needs		X——————X	
Pruning	X——————X		
Staking		X	
Maintenance		X	

Acer pensylvanicum – ACERACEAE
Snakebark Maple, Moose-wood

Origin Eastern North America. A hardy deciduous tree.

Uses
The Snakebark Maple is best used as a single specimen, or in groups of two or more.

Description
Dimensions Average ultimate size 4.5–6m (15–20ft) high by 3–3.5m (10–12ft) wide. Under good conditions trees can grow half as high again.
Rate of growth Moderate.
Life span Usually 70 or more years.
Habit Usually erect, not spreading, with conspicuous stems.
Leaves Fairly large, pinkish when opening, becoming green and then turning yellow in autumn.
Flowers Yellowish, rather inconspicuous flowers, sparsely produced in pendent racemes.
Fruits Winged nuts, brownish when mature, occur in pendulous racemes.
Bark Green when young, later becoming marked with white lines or striations.

Features
The bark on trunk and stem is unusual and provides year-round interest, added to which is the leaf colouring in late spring and autumn.
In all but the most exposed situations this tree is wind-firm.
Pollution Fairly tolerant of normal town conditions.
Non-poisonous.

Variety
Acer pensylvanicum 'Erythrocladum'. Has the added attraction of colourful young shoots in autumn. After leaf fall the young growths turn bright crimson.

Requirements
Position Sheltered but sunny situations in lowland areas of the mild temperate zone suit this tree. It tolerates shade when young.
Soil Slightly acid, well drained loams, pH 6.3–6.8, are close to the ideal.

Notes on culture
Planting Trees up to 3m (10ft) high should be planted between autumn and spring. Stake and tie all trees over 1m (3½ft) high until well established.
Space Give these trees a minimum area of 3m (10ft) diameter for development, and the same distance again from buildings.

Pruning Prune to form the initial framework. Little is required thereafter, but the lower branches may be removed to allow the stems to be seen.
Underplanting When established this tree may be underplanted with low ground-cover plants. If it is underplanted with shrubs part of the bark, which is the chief attraction, is lost from view. However, plants and shrubs which flourish in neutral or near-neutral soils, such as dwarf forms of Berberis and Mahonia, associate well with the Snakebark Maple.

46

Pest and disease control   Minimal, being carried out only if and when attacks are imminent. Occasional caterpillar infestations can be checked with fenitrothion, and mildew and tar spot are controlled by benomyl or copper sprays respectively.

Propagation   By seeds sown in autumn; grafting in spring; or layering in autumn.

Season of interest	Winter	Spring	Late spring	Summer	Late summer	Autumn
In full leaf			X————		—X	
Autumn colour				—	X———	—X
Flowers						
Fruits						
Bark and stem	X————					———X

The following five characteristics determine to a great extent the amount of attention a specific tree requires.

	When planted	5 years	20 years
Height	1·8m	3·0m	4·5m
Width	750mm	1·8m	2·5m
Root spread		2·5m	3·5m
Hardiness	B/C	B	B
Wind-firm		2/3	2

Plant care profile

	Minimum	Average	High
Site needs	X———		—X
Soil needs	X		
Pruning	X———		—X
Staking	X		
Maintenance	X		

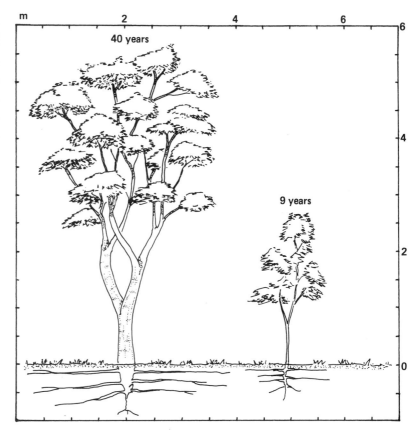

Acer platanoides – ACERACEAE
Norway Maple

Origin Europe.
A hardy deciduous tree.

Uses
The Norway Maple is excellent as a specimen tree on lawns, or in large shrubberies. It is inclined to be too large for small gardens.

Description
Dimensions Average ultimate size 9–12m (30–40ft) high by 4.5–7.5m (15–25ft) wide.
Rate of growth Rapid in the early years, slowing down according to age and site conditions.
Life span Trees reach maturity at 60–70 years old, but can live for double or treble that period.
Habit An upright tree, taller than broad, spreading with age where space and light permit.
Leaves One of the main features. Lobed, brighter green than those of the Sycamore, which they resemble. In autumn the leaves turn to shades of rusty reds, yellows and browns.
Flowers Attractive bright greenish-yellow flowers appear in clusters, dotted among the branches, before the leaves open in the spring.
Fruits The samarae or seeds are typically winged as with most Maples, hang in clusters, and are brownish in colour when ripe.
Bark Dark grey-brown.

Features
This Maple has many virtues. It can be vigorous, is wind-firm, is very hardy, and the foliage retains its attraction through the growing season.
The seasons of interest are mainly from spring to autumn. Remarkably tolerant of town conditions and thrives in most soils. Usually makes a large, handsome tree.
Pollution Tolerates higher pollution level than most trees.
Non-poisonous.

Varieties
Acer platanoides 'Columnare'. Columnar in outline, with upright-growing branches.
Acer platanoides 'Crimson King'. Purple-crimson leaves.
Acer platanoides 'Drummondii'. Green leaves, distinctively margined with white.
Acer platanoides 'Laciniatum' (Eagle's Claw Maple). Smaller, more upright tree than type. Leaf lobes tapering, curved and claw-like.
Acer platanoides 'Reitenbachii'. Green leaves which turn red in autumn.
Acer platanoides 'Schwedleri'. Leaves bright red or pinkish in spring, later turning green.

Requirements
Position This Maple and its varieties can be planted in most cool or mild parts of the temperate zone. They are very hardy, but varieties grown mainly for the leaf colour need protection from cold, drying winds. Sunny, sheltered situations are ideal, but some light shade for part only of each day can be tolerated.
Soil Should be deep, well drained, of average fertility, cool and yet reasonably moisture-retentive. A pH of 6.5–6.8 seems to suit best, but neutral or slightly alkaline, up to pH 7.2, can be tolerated.

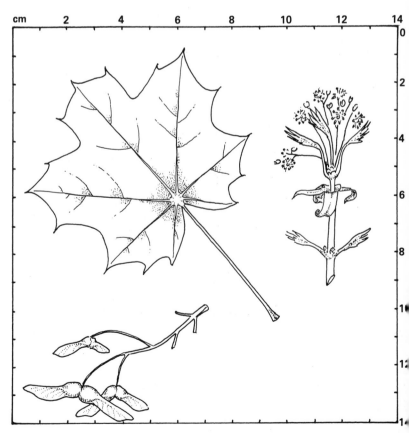

The outline and fresh spring foliage of Japanese Maple in the foreground, and the *Acer pseudoplatanus* 'Brilliantissimum' centre, complement and yet contrast with each other

The shape and colour of individual leaves can be interesting and attractive when viewed closely, as with these of *Robinia pseudoacacia* 'Frizia' as well as when seen from afar

Season, time of day and sunlight play their part when considering trees. In this wooded setting, the spring colouring in soft greens, golds and purple is enhanced by long shadows

In this summer scene are some effective colour combinations. Purple-leaved *Prunus* 'Pissardii' provide a background for the grey Willow-leaf Pear. The yellowy green of *Robina* 'Frizia' stands out from the other trees

Notes on culture

Planting Trees up to 3m (10ft) high should be planted from autumn to spring. Stake and tie larger specimens, 1.5m (5ft) and over, until firmly rooted.

Space Allow an area of 6m (20ft) minimum diameter, and the same distance again from buildings. Avoid planting closer than 4.5m (15ft) to surface water drains, as roots of this species especially could cause problems.

Pruning This consists of removing weak and badly placed shoots to form a well shaped framework of branches. Subsequent requirements are negligible, nothing is necessary beyond cutting out crossing, badly placed or diseased branches.

Underplanting While barberries and hypericums can look and grow well under the branches, plants which require considerable moisture such as fuchsias may suffer unduly in dry districts where the competition for soil water is intense.

Pest and disease control Aphids which cause sticky honey dew and sooty moulds on leaves are sometimes troublesome in warm districts. Spray with malathion. Mildew can appear in hot, dry seasons – spray with benomyl.

Propagation By seeds sown in autumn. Named varieties by grafting on seedling rootstocks in spring, or budding in summer.

Plant care profile

	Minimum	Average	High
Site needs		X	
Soil needs		X	
Pruning	X———X		
Staking	X———X		
Maintenance	X		

Season of interest	Winter	Spring	Late spring	Summer	Late summer	Autumn
In full leaf			X————	————	——X	
Autumn colour				—	X———	—X
Flowers		X—X				
Fruits						
Bark and stem						

The following five characteristics determine to a great extent the amount of attention a specific tree requires.

	When planted	5 years	20 years
Height	2·1 m	4·0 m	7·5 m
Width	900 mm	2·0 m	3·5 m
Root spread		3·0 m	5·0 m
Hardiness	A/B	A	A
Wind-firm		1/2	1

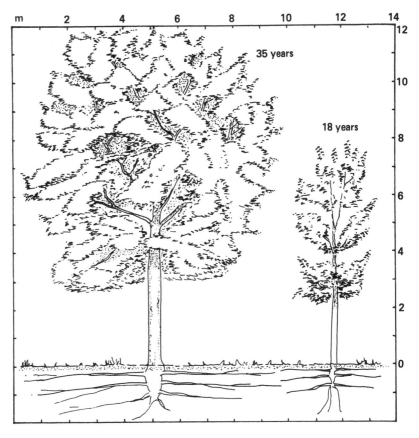

35 years

18 years

49

Acer pseudoplatanus – ACERACEAE
Sycamore, Sycamore Maple

Origin   Europe.
A very hardy deciduous tree.

Uses

The Sycamore may be used in coastal areas or inland, on low or even high ground as a screen or shelter. The use of the type is best reserved for larger gardens or open spaces in residential areas. The varieties can be seen to better effect as specimen trees on lawns or in shrubberies.

Description

Dimensions   Average ultimate size 10.5–12m (35–40ft) high by 4.5–6m (15–20ft) wide, and in ideal conditions can almost double these dimensions. However, it is more usually seen as short, sometimes stunted trees on exposed sites.
Rate of growth   Rapid in early years, reducing to moderate and slow with age.
Life span   Trees reach maturity at 50–60 years old, but can live up to 200 years and over.
Habit   A round-headed tree.
Leaves   A dull green, turning yellowish or brown shades in autumn.
Flowers   Inconspicuous.
Fruits   The samarae or seeds, which appear in late summer in bunches, are freely produced but are a brownish-grey when ripe and not very colourful.
Bark   Inconspicuous at first, becoming attractive later.

Features

The Sycamore is wind-firm, very hardy and can tolerate conditions in which other kinds of tree would not survive. The seeds can be rather a nuisance. Excellent where vegetation is difficult to establish. The varieties are more colourful than the species.
Pollution   Remarkably tolerant, growing where other kinds fail.
Non-poisonous.

Varieties

Acer pseudoplatanus 'Brilliantissimum'. Leaves bright pink on opening in spring.
Acer pseudoplatanus 'Corstorphinense'. Foliage pale yellow, turning to gold.
Acer pseudoplatanus purpureum. Purple foliage.
Acer pseudoplatanus 'Worleei'. Yellow leaves from spring to summer.

Requirements

Position   The sycamore will grow and thrive in most parts of the cool temperate zone. The largest specimens are to be found in cool, mild districts on open, sunny but sheltered sites.
Soil   These trees can be found growing on different soil types from acid to alkaline. The best results are to be obtained from deep, cool, well drained medium loams that are neutral or slightly alkaline, pH 7–7.2.

Notes on culture

Planting   Plant trees up to 4m (13ft) high between autumn and spring. Stake and tie all trees over 1m (3½ft) high at planting until firmly rooted.

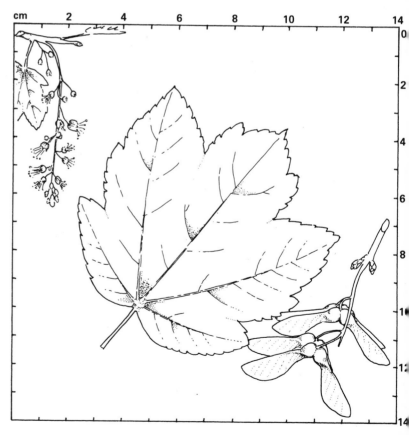

Space Give a minimum area of 6m (20ft) diameter, and at least the same distance again from buildings.

Pruning Cut out badly placed branches and those with a narrow crotch to form an initial crown framework of branches. Subsequent treatment is negligible, except for removing crossing branches.

Underplanting Shrubs and ground-cover plants can be successfully underplanted, but like Norway Maple, the Sycamore can provide keen competition for food and moisture.

Pest and disease control Aphids and leaf gall are the most common pests of sycamore. Spray with malathion against aphids, leave leaf gall to die out. Diseases which can sometimes prove troublesome are: coral spot fungus, appearing as bright pink, cushion-like dots on infected shoots; honey fungus, which can kill trees of all ages; mildew, a white covering on leaves which sometimes appears in hot, dry conditions. Cut out dead shoots for coral spot; dig out dead trees for honey fungus; spray with benomyl against mildew. Tar spot, which occurs as dark blotches, often with yellow margins, on leaves is as a rule more unsightly than serious, but can be checked with copper sprays if necessary.

Propagation By seeds sown in autumn. Named varieties by grafting on seedling rootstocks in spring and budding in summer.

Plant care profile

	Minimum	Average	High
Site needs	X———X		
Soil needs	X———X		
Pruning	X		
Staking	X		
Maintenance	X———X		

Season of interest	Winter	Spring	Late spring	Summer	Late summer	Autumn
In full leaf			X———	———	———X	
Autumn colour					X———	———X
Flowers						
Fruits						
Bark and stem						

The following five characteristics determine to a great extent the amount of attention a specific tree requires.

	When planted	5 years	20 years
Height	2·4 m	4·0 m	5·0 m
Width	1·2 m	1·8 m	3·5 m
Root spread		2·5 m	4·5 m
Hardiness	A/B	A	A
Wind-firm		1	1

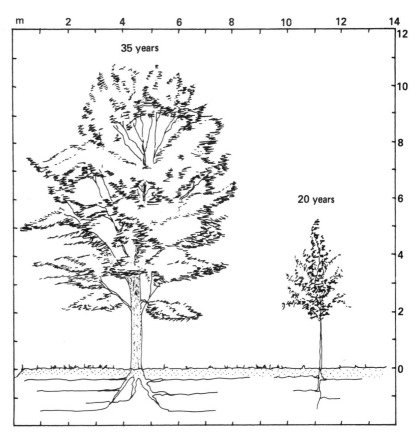

Aesculus x carnea – HIPPOCASTANACEAE

Horse Chestnut, Red Horse Chestnut, Pink Horse Chestnu

Origin Europe.
Considered to be a cross between
A. hippocastanum (Common Horse
Chestnut) and *A. pavia*.
A deciduous tree that is
frost-hardy, but slightly less so than
the Common Horse Chestnut.

Uses
This Horse Chestnut and its
varieties need space and are best
used as specimen trees. They will
provide height and privacy at
maturity as well as quite effectively
deadening noise when in full leaf.

Description
Dimensions Average ultimate size
5–17m (7–23ft) high by 2.5–4m
(8–13ft) wide.
Rate of growth Moderate, similar
to that of the native common
variety in early years, slowing down
with age.
Life span Not known with
certainty but probably over 80
years.
Habit Round-headed or upright.
Leaves Palmate, usually five or
seven dark green lobes, which turn
yellowish then brown in autumn.
Flowers Pink and similar in shape
to those of the Common Horse
Chestnut. They appear usually in
late spring or early summer.
Fruits The crops of seeds or
conkers so popular with
schoolchildren are usually lighter
than those of the Common Horse
Chestnut.
Bark Dark brownish-grey,
sometimes developing
protuberances with age.

Features
Outstanding as a flowering tree,
and more ornamental than the
Common Horse Chestnut, *A. x
carnea* has one or two irritating
habits. There is a tendency for
branches to die off, necessitating
their regular removal. The autumn
leaf fall, though lighter than that of
the native Horse Chestnut, can
cause problems. *A. x carnea* is
wind-firm.
Pollution Remarkably tolerant.
Non-poisonous.

Variety
Aesculus x *carnea* 'Briotii'. Darker
pink flowers, very attractive.

Requirements
Position This Horse Chestnut will
flourish in the mild temperate zone
if it is given a warm, sunny site,
sheltered from cold or strong
winds, which can cause leaf-scorch.
A south-facing aspect is best. It can
be successfully grown in sheltered
situations near the coast.
Soil Although the Chestnut is
tolerant of a range of soil types,
deep, well drained, fertile loam that
is neutral, pH 7, suits it best.

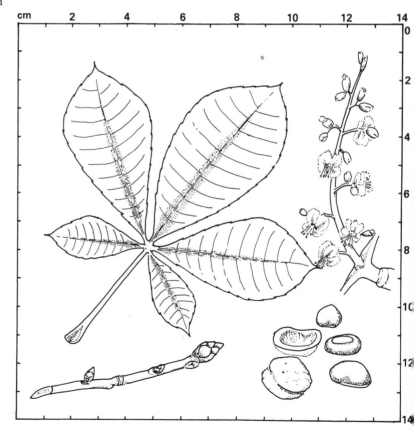

Notes on culture

Planting Trees 1.8–2.5m (6–8ft) high establish more quickly than larger specimens. Standard and half-standard are best. Plant between autumn and spring and stake for year or two until established.

Space Allow room for development. This tree needs a minimum area of 4m (13ft) diameter headroom, plus a similar distance again from buildings.

Pruning Once the crown has been formed maintenance needs are modest, consisting mainly of cutting out dead branches each year.

Underplanting Foliage shrubs are more satisfactory than those which are notable for flowers due to the usually dense canopy of leaves.

Pest and disease control Rarely a problem with these trees.

Propagation By seeds sown when ripe. *A.* x *c.* 'Briotii' by grafting on seed-raised plants during spring; or budding in summer.

Season of interest	Winter	Spring	Late spring	Summer	Late summer	Autumn
In full leaf			X———————	————————	—X	
Autumn colour					X——	—X
Flowers			X—X			
Fruits						
Bark and stem	————————	————————	—X			X—

The following five characteristics determine to a great extent the amount of attention a specific tree requires.

	When planted	5 years	20 years
Height	2·1 m	3·0 m	5·5 m
Width	750 mm	2·0 m	4·5 m
Root spread		3·0 m	5·5 m
Hardiness	B/C	B	B
Wind-firm		1	1

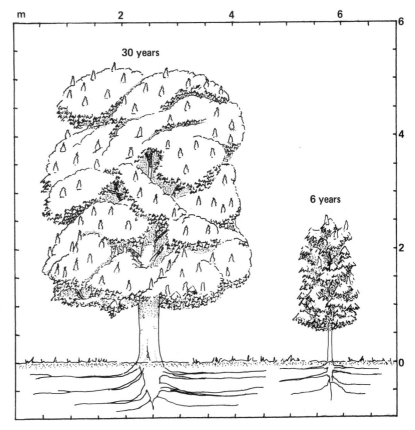

Plant care profile

	Minimum	Average	High
Site needs		X——————X	
Soil needs		X	
Pruning		X——————X	
Staking	X——————X		
Maintenance		X——————X	

Betula pendula – BETULACEAE
Common Silver Birch, European Silver Birch

Origin Arctic and temperate zones of northern hemisphere. One of the hardiest of all deciduous trees.

Uses
This tree is admirable when grown as a specimen or in groups, or in shrubberies.

Description
Dimensions Average size at maturity 6–9m (20–30ft) high by 2.5–3.5m (8–12ft) wide.
Rate of growth Moderate to rapid, depending on variety.
Life span 30–70 years and over. Shallow, dry chalk soils seem to shorten the life span.
Habit Upright pendulous or weeping habit.
Leaves Mid-green ovate or diamond-shaped, and makes a light leaf fall in autumn.
Flowers Pretty yellowish catkins.
Fruits Brownish fruiting catkins with plate-like seeds.
Bark Attractive whitish bark.

Features
The Silver Birch is outstanding for its graceful, light foliage, which allows sunlight to filter through, and the beautiful whitish-barked trunks provide year-round interest. When the tree is leafless during the winter months the delicate network of fine shoots contrasts against the white stems. This tree does not seem to have any serious faults. It is hardy, erect, wind-firm and the leaf fall is only light.
Pollution Fairly tolerant, making a good town tree.
Non-poisonous.

Varieties
There are many different kinds of Birch, some of which are less suitable than others for planting in gardens. A few of the more garden-worthy varieties of *Betula pendula* are given below.
Betula pendula 'Dalecarlica' (Swedish Birch). A graceful, weeping form.
Betula pendula 'Fastigiata'. A fairly narrow, erect form, resembling the Lombardy Poplar in outline.
Betula pendula 'Tristis'. An erect tree but with pendulous branches.
Betula pendula 'Youngii' (Young's Weeping Birch). Forms a globose or vaguely mushroom-shaped weeping tree.

Requirements
Position While Birch can be grown virtually anywhere, better and larger trees are produced in more sheltered situations. Sunny or lightly shaded sites are suitable, though the light-coloured stems stand out even more effectively in sunlight. The birch is as at home in coastal areas as it is inland.
Soil Sandy or medium loams that are acid or neutral, pH 5.5–7 are ideal. Although this tree will grow on dry ground, well drained, moisture-retentive soils are best.

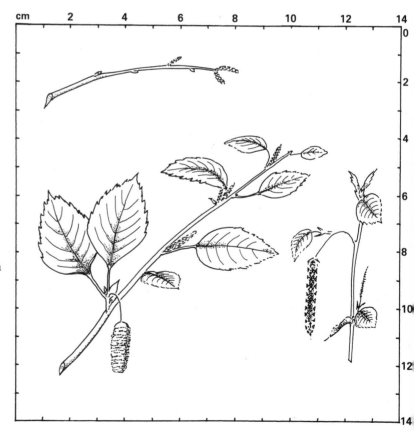

Notes on culture

Planting Trees may be planted when small or up to 3–4m (10–13ft) high. Plant between autumn and spring and stake standard or half-standard trees until they are established.

Space Specimen trees may need up to 7.5m (25ft) or more in diameter. Trees in groups can be planted closer, at 2–3m (7–10ft) apart. Birch is less invasive than many trees and it shuts out less light, but it is best planted at least 6m (20ft) from buildings.

Pruning In formal gardens needs are negligible once the crown has been formed in older trees. In a natural setting, only dead or badly placed branches need to be cut out.

Underplanting Bulbs of various kinds, such as crocus, daffodil and narcissus look well in chalk soils. Heathers, dwarf azaleas and rhododendrons associate well on acid land.

Pest and disease control Rarely a problem.

Propagation By ripe seeds sown in spring. Named varieties by grafting on seed-raised plants also in spring.

Season of interest	Winter	Spring	Late spring	Summer	Late summer	Autumn
In full leaf			X————	————	——X	
Autumn colour					X——	—X
Flowers		X——	—X			
Fruits						
Bark and stem	X——	————	————	————	————	—X—

The following five characteristics determine to a great extent the amount of attention a specific tree requires.

	When planted	5 years	20 years
Height	2·4 m	4·0 m	7·5 m
Width	1·2 m	2·0 m	3·0 m
Root spread		3·0 m	4·0 m
Hardiness	A/B	A	A
Wind-firm		1	1

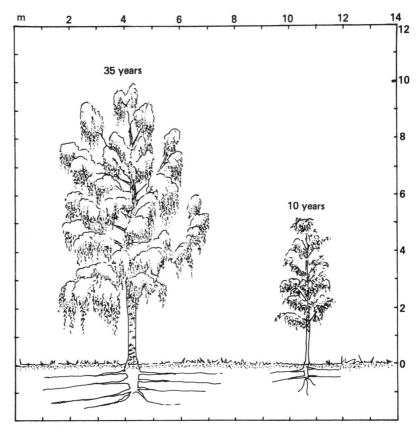

Plant care profile

	Minimum Average High
Site needs	X————X
Soil needs	X————X
Pruning	X
Staking	X————X
Maintenance	X

Carpinus betulus – CARPINACEAE
Common Hornbeam, European Hornbeam

Origin Europe (including
Britain) and Asia Minor.
A hardy deciduous tree.

Uses
C. betulus can be useful for
screening and shelter where space
allows. It is commonly found in
hedgerows in some districts. The
varieties are better suited than the
type for garden purposes, being
used as specimen trees where more
subdued planting effects are
required.

Description
Dimensions Average size at
maturity around 5–8m (17–26ft)
high by 3–4.5m (10–15ft) wide, but
some larger specimens can be seen
in milder temperate areas.
Rate of growth Can vary from
slow to moderate, depending on
local conditions; moderate on good
soils when well eatablished.
Life span Trees can be expected
to live well in excess of 100 years.
Habit A medium-size tree of
upright or rounded form.
Leaves Young trees retain their
leaves in winter. The green summer
foliage turns yellow shades in
autumn, eventually becoming
brown.
Flowers Older trees produce a
display of pendulous yellowish
catkins in late spring.
Fruits Brownish fruiting catkins
with lobed bracts, curious more
than colourful.
Bark Grey bark that becomes
rugged with age.

Features
Well suited for more natural
gardens of medium or large size,
and needs little attention.
Hornbeam is useful and reliable,
being wind-firm and hardy. Some
of its varieties make very desirable
garden trees.
Pollution Fairly tolerant.
Non-poisonous.

Varieties
Carpinus betulus 'Columnaris'. A
fastigiate form, striking in effect.
Carpinus betulus 'Incisa'.
Distinctive, narrow, deeply toothed
leaves.
Carpinus betulus 'Pendula'. A
weeping habit.
Carpinus betulus 'Variegata'.
Variegated foliage, producing a
mottled effect.

Requirements
Position The Hornbeam and its
varieties can be grown successfully
in many parts of the temperate
zone, tolerating more exposed
positions than Beech. They grow
well in sun, which favours a better
display of catkins, but also tolerate
some shade. They are able to
withstand open situations but better
coloured leaves are produced in
more sheltered spots.
Soil Well drained light loams with
a pH of 6.5–7 are good, but this
tree will flourish on most types of
land including even chalk. It can
sometimes prove to be rather large
on heavy, rich, moist loams.

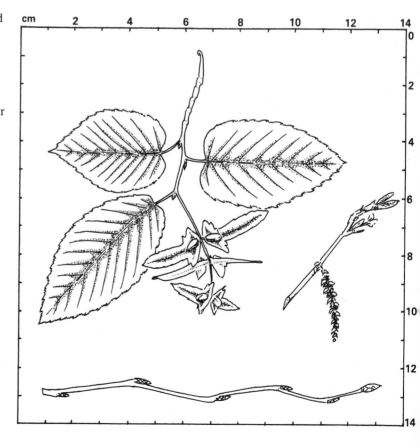

Notes on culture

Planting Can be planted when small or up to 2.5–3m (8–10ft) in height. Plant between autumn and spring and stake all trees until established.

Space On rich, fertile soil allow each tree a clear space, 6m (20ft) in diameter, and half the same distance again from buildings.

Pruning Prune to form the initial crown framework. Very little cutting is needed thereafter.

Underplanting Shrubs or other vegetation planted under Hornbeam will find the competition somewhat severe.

Pest and disease control Occasionally small trees may succumb to honey fungus on land newly cleared of old trees. Dig up any dead stumps and burn before planting. Otherwise Hornbeam is usually trouble-free.

Propagation By stratified seeds sown in spring. Named varieties by grafting indoors in spring.

Season of interest	Winter	Spring	Late spring	Summer	Late summer	Autumn
In full leaf			X————	————	—X	
Autumn colour					X—	X
Flowers			X—X			
Fruits						
Bark and stem	——————	————	—X			X—

The following five characteristics determine to a great extent the amount of attention a specific tree requires.

	When planted	5 years	20 years
Height	2·1 m	3·0m	5·5 m
Width	750 mm	2·5 m	3·5 m
Root spread		3·5 m	4·5 m
Hardiness	A/B	A	A
Wind-firm		1/2	1

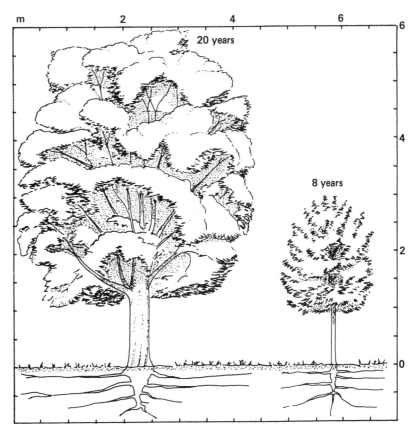

Plant care profile

	Minimum	Average	High
Site needs	X		
Soil needs		X	
Pruning	X————	—X	
Staking	X————	—X	
Maintenance	X		

Catalpa bignonioides – BIGNONIACEAE
Indian Bean Tree

Origin   Eastern North America. A deciduous tree only moderately frost-hardy.

Uses
This tree is seen at its best as a single specimen, rather than planted in a group.

Description
Dimensions   Average ultimate size 6–7.5m (20–25ft) high by 4.5–6m (15–20ft) wide.
Rate of growth   Rather slow.
Life span   80 years and more.
Habit   A broadly rounded tree.
Leaves   Large, green, heart-shaped leaves in summer, becoming yellow in autumn after a hot summer.
Flowers   White and yellow flowers on mature trees during good summers.
Fruits   Curious bean-like pods which remain on the branches long after the leaves fall, giving the tree quite an eerie appearance at dawn or dusk in winter.
Bark   Grey, not particularly striking.

Features
This tree is attractive for the sake of its leaves during the late spring and summer, and the flowers are attractive. It is sturdy and wind-firm, but unfortunately the leaves can quite easily be scorched by wind. The pods, left on trees after leaf drop, are quite distinctive.
Pollution   Fairly tolerant.
Non-poisonous.

Variety
Catalpa bignonioides 'Aurea'. Can be quite striking when carefully sited and well grown. Yellow leaves.

Requirements
Position   This tree grows best in south-facing, sun-drenched, sheltered lowland sites in the mild or warm temperate zone. It needs protection from cold winds, which can cause leaf-scorch, and it should ideally have a long growing season.
Soil   The requirements are more exacting than for some trees. Deep, well drained, fertile loams that are moisture-retentive yet not heavy or clayey are ideal. A neutral soil, pH 7, will suit best. Shallow gravels or stiff clay soils can produce a form of leaf-browning.

Notes on culture
Planting   Preferably plant small trees, up to 2m (7ft) high, in autumn, but specimens up to 2.5–3m (8–10ft) can be successfully moved. Stake and tie larger trees until established.
Space   Provide adequate space for development, not less than 6m (20ft) diameter and the same distance from buildings.
Pruning   Prune to form the initial crown framework. Little is needed thereafter.

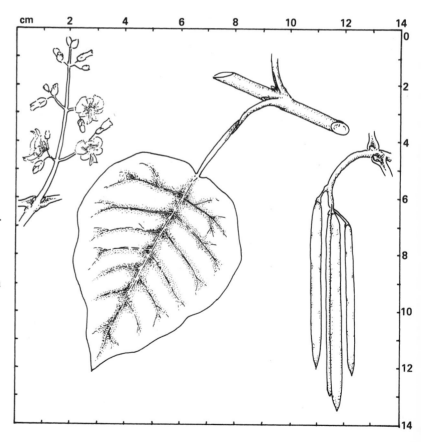

58

Underplanting This tree casts rather too much shade in summer for the satisfactory growth of shrubs or ground-cover plants beneath.
Pest and disease control Given the conditions it needs the Indian Bean Tree suffers from very few problems.
Propagation By cuttings taken in mid-late summer, and the species by spring-sown seeds.

Season of interest	Winter	Spring	Late spring	Summer	Late summer	Autumn
In full leaf				X————	————X	
Autumn colour						
Flowers				X——X		
Fruits	——————X				X—————	————
Bark and stem						

The following five characteristics determine to a great extent the amount of attention a specific tree requires.

	When planted	5 years	20 years
Height	1·5 m	2·5 m	5·0 m
Width	600 mm	2·0 m	4·0 m
Root spread		3·0 m	5·0 m
Hardiness	C	B/C	B/C
Wind-firm		1/2	1

Plant care profile

	Minimum	Average	High
Site needs		X———X	
Soil needs		X———X	
Pruning	X———X		
Staking		X	
Maintenance		X	

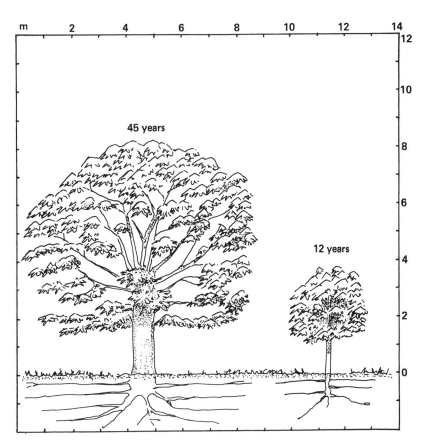

Cercidiphyllum japonicum
False Redbud

Origin   China and Japan.
A moderately hardy deciduous tree.

Uses
C. japonicum is effective as a specimen tree, especially on lawns.

Description
Dimensions   Very variable, but an average ultimate size of 6–9m (20–30ft) high by 4.5–6.5m (15–22ft) wide is usual. Specimens half as large again occur in the tree's natural habitat.
Rate of growth   Moderate in early years, becoming slow.
Life span   Variable up to 60 years and over.
Habit   A spreading tree of elegant proportions. The trunk is often spirally twisted and furrowed.
Leaves   The main attraction of this tree. The leaves open red or reddish and turn green, then in autumn, under good conditions, turn yellow and red. Some strains, however, do not show a marked red autumn coloration.
Flowers   Fairly insignificant, petalless, borne in clusters in spring. Male and female flowers occur on different trees.
Fruits   Purple-brown, often sparce or absent.
Bark   Greyish-brown, not outstanding.

Features
The striking leaf colour is the main attraction of this tree. *C. japonicum* is very hardy in the dormant condition, favouring a continental-type climate. Unfortunately the leaves can be damaged by late spring frost. The tree is wind-firm and stable when trained to a single stem.
Pollution   Tolerance is doubtful. Large specimens occur mainly in rural areas.
Non-poisonous.

Varieties
Although there is some variation in form and colouring there does not appear to be any noteworthy variety readily available, other than *C. j. sinense*, which has much brighter red autumn colouring than the type.

Requirements
Position   Avoid cold districts, planting preferably in mild or warm areas. Sunny but sheltered situations, protected from strong or cold winds, are most suitable.
Soil   A moderately deep, moisture-retentive loam that is neutral or slightly alkaline, pH 7–7.2, gives the best results.

Notes on culture
Planting   Plant small trees, preferably not more than 1.8–2m (6–7ft) high during late autumn. Stake and tie trees until firmly rooted.
Space   Allow an area of 6m (20ft) diameter and the same distance again from any buildings.
Pruning   This consists of removing all but one vertical growths in young trees, where the main stem has formed two or more shoots of equal vigour. Cut out any badly placed stems to form the initial crown. Subsequently little or no pruning is necessary.

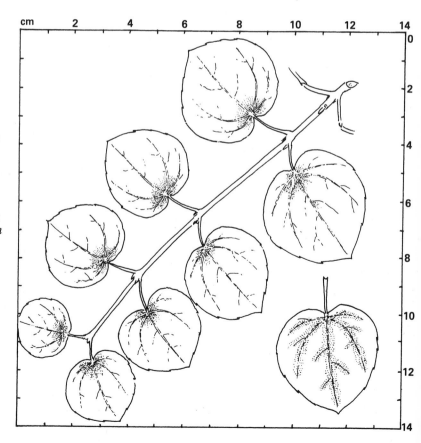

Underplanting   With the exception of low ground cover, this is not particularly effective with specimen trees.

Pest and disease control   Rarely a problem.

Propagation   By seeds sown in spring.

Season of interest	Winter	Spring	Late spring	Summer	Late summer	Autumn
In full leaf			X———	————	——X	
Autumn colour					X——	—X
Flowers						
Fruits						
Bark and stem	———————	————	——X			X—

The following five characteristics determine to a great extent the amount of attention a specific tree requires.

	When planted	5 years	20 years
Height	1·2 m	1·8 m	4·0 m
Width	600 mm	1·2 m	2·5 m
Root spread		2·0 m	3·5 m
Hardiness	C	C	B/C
Wind-firm		2	1/2

Plant care profile

	Minimum	Average	High
Site needs		X——X	
Soil needs		X——X	
Pruning		X	
Staking		X	
Maintenance		X	

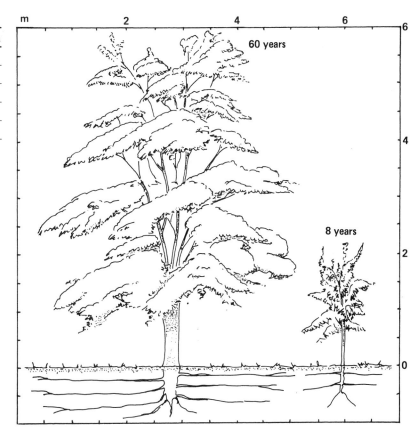

61

Cercis siliquastrum – LEGUMINOSAE
Judas Tree or Redbud

Origin Southern Europe and Asia. A deciduous tree, only moderately frost-hardy.

Uses
C. siliquastrum may be grown as a specimen, in a group, in shrubberies or against a wall. The flowers can be used in salads.

Description
Dimensions Variable, but when mature can reach 4.5–6m (15–20ft) high by 3–4.5m (10–15ft) or more wide.
Rate of growth Usually slow.
Life span This tree can live for 100 years or more.
Habit A small, rounded tree, sometimes spreading.
Leaves Attractive heart-shaped but fairly small leaves of mid-green, without any pronounced autumn colouring, except after hot summers.
Flowers Pea-shaped and rosy purple, opening in spring before the leaves and creating a charming pinkish haze effect among the bare branches.
Fruits Green pods, resembling those of peas, but turning pinkish-purple shades when ripe.
Bark Dark grey, often overlaid with green algal growth.

Features
The main feature of this tree is the appearance of the flowers before the leaves unfold, but it has considerable appeal from the spring when the flowers open to leaf fall in autumn. The seed pods add interest in late summer.
Pollution Fairly tolerant of normal town conditions.
Non-poisonous.

Variety
Cercis siliquastrum 'Alba'. A white-flowered form.

Requirements
Position *C. siliquastrum* needs a warm, sheltered site in full sun, not subject to late frosts. While the tree itself can stand a fair amount of frost, unfortunately the flowers cannot.
Soil Warm, well drained but moisture-retentive ground containing some chalk and with a pH around 7 suits this tree.

Notes on culture
Planting These trees resent being moved and should be planted in autumn when quite small. Container-grown plants suffer less when being transplanted than plants grown in open ground. In either case one or two canes and twine are all that is needed by way of support.

Space As this tree is slow-growing and not invasive by nature, in a cool site it can safely be planted to within 600mm (2ft) of a large expanse of wall. Give trees planted in more open situations space to grow, say 3–4m (10–13ft) diameter.
Pruning After the formative stage this is only occasionally needed to keep trees in shape. Cut out crossing or badly placed shoots or branches. Wall-trained trees may require more frequent attention to maintain shape and form.
Underplanting Low-ground cover can be successfully used, but taller shrubs are best avoided for trees to be seen to maximum effect.

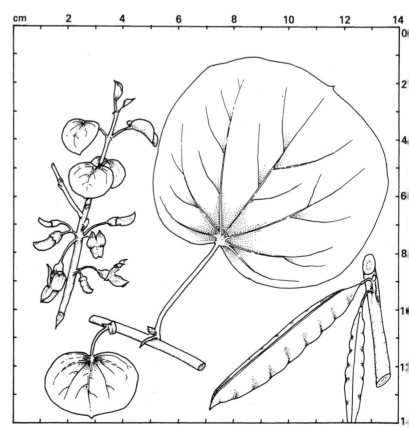

Pest and disease control   This tree is only infrequently bothered by pests or diseases. The coral spot fungus sometimes attacks old trees, and affected parts are best removed promptly.

Propagation   Usually by means of layers, pegged down in autumn or spring. Grafting named varieties in spring is also used. The species can be raised from seeds, sown in spring.

Season of interest	Winter	Spring	Late spring	Summer	Late summer	Autumn
In full leaf			X———	———	———X	
Autumn colour					X——	——X
Flowers		X——	——X			
Fruits						
Bark and stem						

The following five characteristics determine to a great extent the amount of attention a specific tree requires.

	When planted	5 years	20 years
Height	1·2 m	2·5 m	4·0 m
Width	600 mm	1·2 m	3·5 m
Root spread		2·0 m	4·5 m
Hardiness	C	C	C
Wind-firm		2	2

Plant care profile

	Minimum	Average	High
Site needs	X——	——X	
Soil needs	X——	——X	
Pruning		X	
Staking		X	
Maintenance		X	

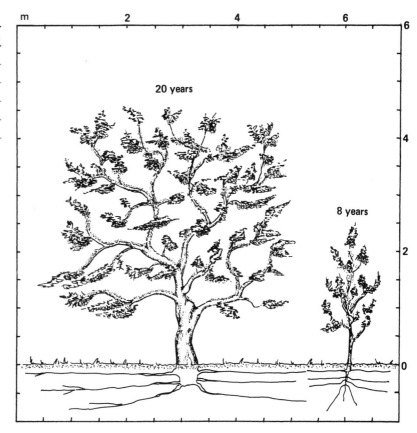

Cotoneaster frigidus – ROSACEAE
Tree Cotoneaster

Origin Himalayas.
A semi-evergreen tree or shrub which is moderately frost-hardy but in cool temperate situations can be deciduous.

Uses
These Cotoneasters may be planted as specimen trees or, if space allows, in groups.

Description
Dimensions Average ultimate size 6m (20ft) high by 3–4.5m (10–15ft) wide.
Rate of growth Rapid when young, slowing to moderate.
Life span Trees of 40–60 years old are not uncommon.
Habit A small flat-topped or upright tree.
Leaves Mid- to dark green, those on the lower branches persisting until spring.
Flowers White, produced in clusters in spring.
Fruits An outstanding autumn display of scarlet berries. In country districts, where birds have alternative fruits to devour, these can persist until well into winter.
Bark Medium brownish-grey often with green covering of algal growth especially in area of high humidity.

Features
The brilliance of the crimson clusters of berries is the main attraction. The seasons of interest are spring, summer and autumn and if the fruits are left by the birds on into early winter. These Cotoneasters are sturdy and wind-firm. The fruits are harmless to children.
Pollution Tolerant, well suited to town situations.
Non-poisonous.

Variety
Cotoneaster frigidus 'Fructuluteo'. Most conspicuous creamy-yellow berries in autumn.

Requirements
Position This tree does best in an open, sunny situation in a mild or warm area. It needs to be sheltered from strong or cold winds.
Soil Well drained loams that are neutral or nearly so, having a pH around 7 suit this tree best, but it can tolerate chalk soil. The ground should preferably be fertile, deep and not inclined to dry out excessively.

Notes on culture
Planting Plant in autumn or spring, either as small plants or when 2.5–3m (8–10ft) high. Stake and tie all trees until they are firmly established.

Space Allow about 4m (13ft) diameter space, half that area if two or more planted in a group, and avoid planting closer to buildings than 3–4m (10–13ft).
Pruning Limit the stems to a single trunk and form a well spaced framework for the crown. This will then need the occasional trim to keep it in shape.
Underplanting Shrubs grow without much difficulty beneath this tree, as it does not compete too fiercely for food, light and moisture.

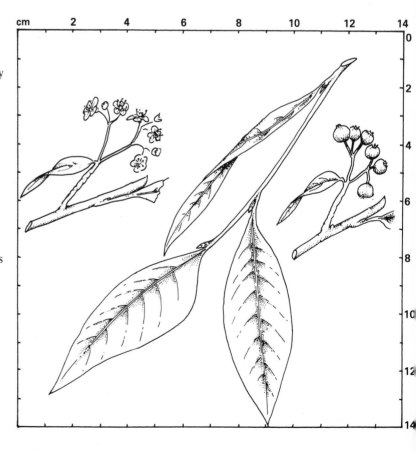

Pest and disease control Aphids and scale insects can be controlled by malathion sprays. Birds are the biggest menace, especially near large towns, where they often clear the berries by late autumn. Fire blight attacks can be troublesome.
Propagation By seeds sown in spring; cuttings of young growth in late summer; or layering in autumn.

Season of interest	Winter	Spring	Late spring	Summer	Late summer	Autumn
In full leaf	——X		X—			
Autumn colour						
Flowers			X—X			
Fruits	⊢X				X—	
Bark and stem						

The following five characteristics determine to a great extent the amount of attention a specific tree requires.

	When planted	5 years	20 years
Height	1·8 m	2·5 m	4·0 m
Width	750 mm	2·5 m	3·5 m
Root spread		3·5 m	4·5 m
Hardiness	B/C	B/C	B/C
Wind-firm		2/3	2

Plant care profile

	Minimum Average High
Site needs	X——X
Soil needs	X
Pruning	X——X
Staking	X——X
Maintenance	X——X

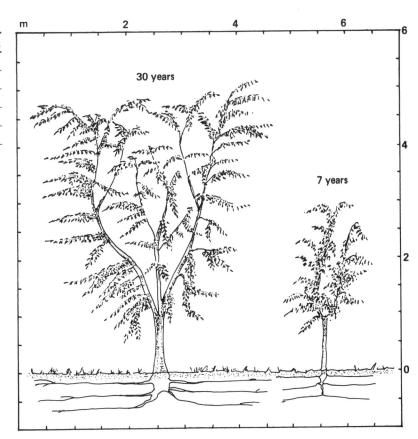

65

Crataegus crus-galli – ROSACEAE
Cockspur Thorn

Origin   Eastern North America.
A hardy deciduous tree or shrub.

Uses
Although Thorns are sometimes used to provide shelter this variety is best used as a specimen tree. The attention required to keep the tree in shape makes it less suitable than others for use in shrubberies.

Description
Dimensions   Average ultimate size 4.5–6m (15–20ft) or more high by as much wide.
Rate of growth   Slow to put on height but rapidly thickens out.
Life span   Can be well in excess of 100 years.
Habit   Forms round to wide-spreading crown of branches.
Leaves   Ovate, green at first, turning to scarlet and crimson shades in autumn.
Flowers   White flowers produced in groups or clusters in spring or summer.
Fruits   Scarlet berries or haws in autumn.
Bark   Mid-grey on trunk.

Features
The Cockspur Thorn is armed with formidable spikes on the shoots and branches. The seasons of colour and interest extend from spring or summer with the flowers, continuing with the autumn tints and berries which last well into winter. This tree has very few bad habits, but there is a noticeable tendency to the formation of a thick, impenetrable crown; and also an inclination to lean away from the prevailing wind, particulary with some grafted specimens.
Pollution   Tolerant of town conditions.
Non-poisonous.

Variety
Crataegus crus-galli pyracanthifolia.   An attractive, small, thornless tree, producing branches that grow more nearly horizontal than those of the type.

Requirements
Position   Being really hardy, the Cockspur Thorns can be grown almost anywhere in the temperate zone. However, they grow best in sheltered situations in the sun, although they will tolerate light shade. Exposed, windy sites are best avoided, because of the tendency to develop a leaning posture.
Soil   These trees are fairly tolerant of varying conditions, but deep, stiff, fertile loams that are neutral, pH 7, and do not dry out are close to the ideal.

Notes on culture
Planting   Plant trees up to 3m (10ft) high between leaf fall and the start of growth in the spring. Stake and tie until established.
Space   Give this Thorn space to develop a well shaped crown. Allow single specimens an area of 6m (20ft) diameter and avoid planting closer to buildings or walls than about 4.5m (15ft).
Pruning   With young trees develop a well shaped framework of branches by cutting out badly placed or weak shoots. Trim mature trees into shape and regularly, every two years or so, thin out crossing and chafing branches.

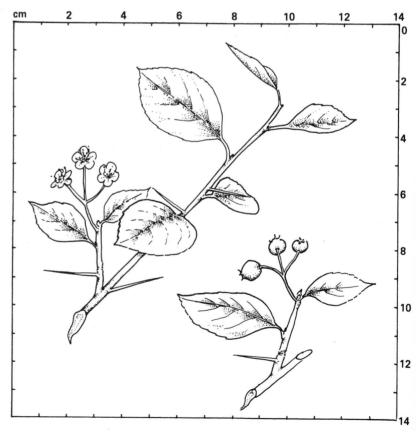

Underplanting Shrubs and ground cover plants can be successfully grown under the branches of trees, but leave working space for pruning.

Pest and disease control
Caterpillars sometimes devour the foliage, but can be checked by spraying with derris or fenitrothion. Fireblight, causing drying and blackening of foliage and withering of berries occurs sometimes. Cut out and burn affected parts. Leaf-spot and mildew can be checked by spraying with a copper fungicide.

Propagation By seeds sown in spring. Named varieties by grafting in spring.

Season of interest	Winter	Spring	Late spring	Summer	Late summer	Autumn
In full leaf			X—————		—————X	
Autumn colour					X———	—X
Flowers		X—X				
Fruits	—X				X———	—
Bark and stem						

The following five characteristics determine to a great extent the amount of attention a specific tree requires.

	When planted	5 years	20 years
Height	2·4 m	3·5 m	4·0 m
Width	1·0 m	2·5 m	4·0 m
Root spread		3·5 m	5·0 m
Hardiness	A / B	A	A
Wind-firm		3	2/3

Plant care profile

	Minimum Average High
Site needs	X————X
Soil needs	X
Pruning	X————X
Staking	X————X
Maintenance	X——X

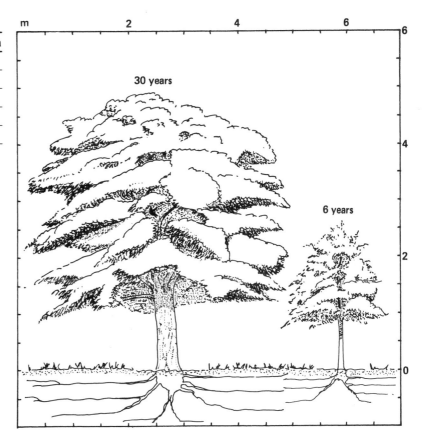

30 years

6 years

Crataegus oxyacantha – ROSACEAE
Hawthorn, May, English Hawthorn

Origin Europe (including Britain) and northern hemisphere. One of the hardiest deciduous trees.

Uses
C. oxyacantha and its varieties make first-class specimen trees, and where space allows two or more can be grouped together.

Description
Dimensions Average ultimate size 6m (20ft) high by about 5m (17ft) wide.
Rate of growth Fairly rapid in early years, becoming slower with age.
Life span Trees can be expected to live for 100 years or more.
Habit Usually round-headed.
Leaves Glossy, medium green in summer, with dull crimson or yellow shades in autumn.
Flowers Usually a splendid show of blossom during late spring, lasting for about two or three weeks from bud stage to petal fall.
Fruits Scarlet-crimson berries or haws in autumn and early winter.
Bark Grey-brown, furrowed and flaking with mature trees.

Features
Extreme hardiness, and the regular autumn display of scarlet-crimson berries are major attractions, as are the scented whitish flowers. Some named varieties of Hawthorn can develop quite a lean, but given a modicum of shelter, staking and tying this need present no great problem. Some varieties with double flowers, provide a longer season of summer flowering, but often have a lighter crop of berries in autumn.
Pollution One of the most resistant, excellent for planting in towns.
Non-poisonous.

Varieties
Crataegus oxyacantha 'Aurea'. Yellowish-green leaves.
Crataegus oxyacantha 'Paul's Scarlet'. A very popular double form with scarlet flowers.
Crataegus oxyacantha 'Plena'. A form with double white flowers.
Crataegus oxyacantha 'Rosea'. Single pink flowers.
Crataegus oxyacantha 'Rosea Flore Pleno'. A double-flowered version of 'Rosea'.

Requirements
Position Given reasonable soil and other conditions the Hawthorn will grow in most parts of the temperate zone and in coastal as well as inland areas. In spite of its hardiness, however, this tree will benefit by protection from freezing or strong prevailing winds, as these conditions not only adversely affect leaves and flowers for one season but progressivily cause trees to become lopsided and unbalanced, so that they develop quite a lean. Sunny situations favour flowering, good autumn leaf colour and fruiting, but some light shade for part of the day is tolerated.

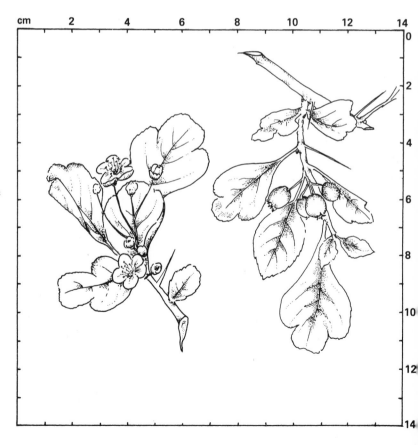

Soil The Hawthorn will thrive in a wide variety of soils, but extremes of moisture or dryness are best avoided. Heavy loams that are well drained and yet retain moisture are excellent, and have a pH range of 6–7.5.

Notes on culture

Planting Trees up to 3m (10ft) high should be planted between autumn and spring. Stake and keep tied until firmly established.

Space Allow Hawthorns about 5m (17ft) diameter space and the same distance from any buildings.

Pruning This chiefly consists of forming a framework of branches. Thereafter all that is necessary is trimming to maintain shape, cutting out or shortening inward-growing or crossing branches.

Underplanting Hawthorns when grown as standards can be underplanted with shrubs to good effect.

Pest and disease control Rarely needed. If necessary caterpillars may be checked by a derris or fenitrothion spray, mildew by spraying with benomyl.

Propagation By seed sown in spring. Named varieties by grafting on seedling stocks of *C. monogyna* in early spring; or budding on similar stocks in late summer.

Season of interest	Winter	Spring	Late spring	Summer	Late summer	Autumn
In full leaf		X—	——	——	—X	
Autumn colour					X—	—X
Flowers			X—X			
Fruits	——	—X			X—	——
Bark and stem						

The following five characteristics determine to a great extent the amount of attention a specific tree requires.

	When planted	5 years	20 years
Height	2·4 m	3·5 m	4·5 m
Width	900 mm	2·0 m	3·5 m
Root spread		3·0 m	4·5 m
Hardiness	A/B	A	A
Wind-firm		2/3	2

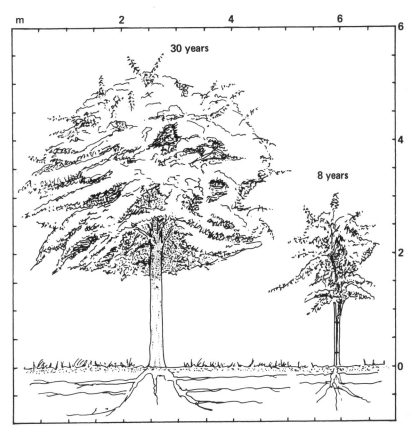

Plant care profile

	Minimum	Average	High
Site needs		X	
Soil needs	X—	—X	
Pruning		X—	—X
Staking		X—	—X
Maintenance		X	

Davidia involucrata – DAVIDIACEAE
Pocket-handkerchief Tree, Ghost Tree

Origin   Western China.
A deciduous tree, moderately hardy in lowland areas.

Uses
The Pocket-handkerchief Tree is seen to best effect as a specimen tree on a lawn, or planted close to shrubs.

Description
Dimensions   Under reasonable conditions can reach 5–7m (17–23ft) high by 3–5m (10–17ft) wide at maturity.
Rate of growth   Slow to moderate.
Life span   Trees of 40 years and over are known.
Habit   Upright.
Leaves   Bright green becoming darker, roughly heart shaped.
Flowers   Large, whitish, petal-like bracts open to reveal small, ball-like flower clusters. The Pocket-handkerchief Tree can flower quite early in life, when only ten–eighteen years old.
Fruits   Green, pear-shaped often with purplish-blue bloom.
Bark   Insignificant.

Features
The major feature of this tree is the petal-like bracts, each of which resembles a handkerchief. A tree when covered with bracts, usually in late spring or early summer, is a most impressive sight. The chief disadvantage of this or any other Davidia is the frost-tender leaves, which prevent its wider distribution.
Pollution   Fairly tolerant.
Non-poisonous.

Variety
Davidia vilmoriniana   Smooth leaves.

Requirements
Position   One of the important needs of this tree is to avoid late spring frosts and cold freezing winds, as the leaves are very frost-tender. The site should be in a mild or warm area, sheltered and sunny, with preferably a south- or west-facing aspect.
Soil ·   A well drained loam, slightly acid to neutral, pH 6–7, approaches the ideal. Deep, moist, fertile ground is best, as it is important that trees should not be allowed to dry out.

Notes on culture
Planting   Plant small trees, up to 2m (7ft) high, preferably in autumn. Stake and tie. Larger specimens do not move well.
Space   Allow a minimum area of 5m (17ft) diameter, and a similar distance from buildings.
Pruning   This consists of shaping the crown initially. Little or no cutting is needed later.
Underplanting   This tree associates well with carefully chosen dwarf shrubs such as Berberis, but low-growing ground cover of cotoneaster, can be effective.

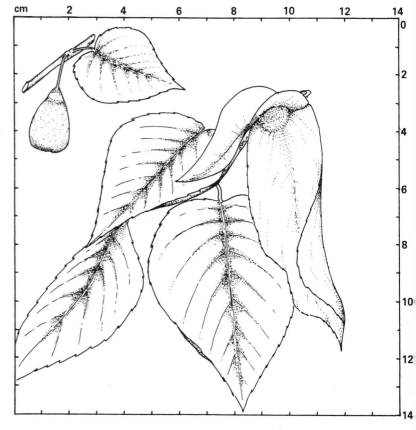

Pest and disease control Rarely necessary. Honey fungus may occur in some situations. Dig out dead tree stumps to remove source of infection.

Propogation Can be propagated by seeds sown in autumn in a cold frame, but this needs a lot of patience: 18–30 months to germinate is not uncommon. Cuttings taken in late summer are more reliable and quicker.

Season of interest	Winter	Spring	Late spring	Summer	Late summer	Autumn
In full leaf			X——————————————X			
Autumn colour						
Flowers			X————————X			
Fruits						
Bark and stem						

The following five characteristics determine to a great extent the amount of attention a specific tree requires.

	When planted	5 years	20 years
Height	1·5 m	3·0 m	4·5 m
Width	600 mm	1·5 m	3·5 m
Root spread		2·5 m	4·5 m
Hardiness	C	B/C	B/C
Wind-firm		2/3	2

Plant care profile

	Minimum	Average	High
Site needs	X——————X		
Soil needs	X——————X		
Pruning	X		
Staking	X		
Maintenance	X		

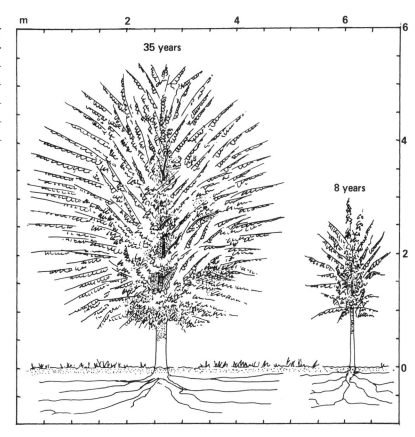

Eucalyptus gunnii – MYRTACEAE
Cider Gum, Blue Gum

Origin   Tasmania and Southern Australia.
A moderately hardy evergreen tree.

Uses
As a specimen tree this is different in its colour effects from other broad-leaved types but unless pollarded, it is more suited to the larger garden. The prunings are often much sought after by flower arrangers.

Description
Dimensions   Variable, being dependent on site and location. Under ideal conditions can reach a size of up to 12m (40ft) high by 4.5m (15ft) wide in 30 years.
Rate of growth   Rapid to moderate, slowing with age.
Life span   Variable, but trees start to decline after 30–40 years.
Habit   Upright and fairly open except when the tree is pollarded, which encourages a more dense head.
Leaves   The young leaves range from blue-green to silvery white in the juvenile stage, becoming darker blue or blue-green in the second and subsequent years. The adult leaves developing from the second season onwards, are long and narrow, unlike the rounded juvenile form, and are blue or blue-green.
Flowers   Scented whitish flowers during the late summer.
Fruits   Urn-shaped, woody, not particulary attractive.
Bark   Pale green or cream, turning grey.

Features
This Gum is notable for its rapid growth when young, the attractive and unusual evergreen foliage, and the fragrant flowers. The scented foliage is much valued for floral arrangements.
Pollution   Moderately tolerant, but the foliage becomes blackened with soot.
Non-poisonous.

Variety
Eucalyptus gunnii whittinghamensis. Considered to be superior to the type, being slightly hardier and more glaucous. Some authorities now consider that this varietal name is no longer valid, but is sometimes offered for sale as this.

Requirements
Position   Planting is best confined to the mild or warm temperate areas. Sheltered, warm, sunny sites protected from strong winds are most suitable. Can be successfully grown in a sheltered position near the coast.
Soil   Well drained, deep, light loams that are neutral or nearly so, with a pH around 7, are best.

Notes on culture
Planting   Seedling trees should be set out in late spring after all danger of keen frost has passed. Stout supports and ties are necessary for three or four years, to prevent wind rock. During this time the trees can grow as much as 4–5m (13–17ft).
Space   Allow a minimum area of 6m (20ft) diameter for each tree, and a similar distance from buildings. These measurements may be reduced by one-third for pollarded specimens.

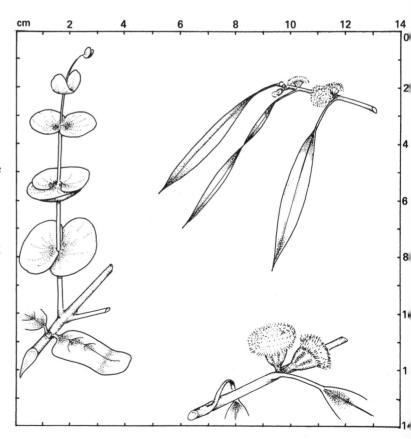

Two flowering chestnuts display their spring glory in majestic fashion: a white Common Horse Chestnut and a Red Chestnut on the right

Autumn tints can be as effective as flowers, a point well demonstrated by the brilliant colouring of the Japanese Maple in the foreground

The leaves of *Catalpa bignonioides*
'Aurea', purple at first, turning yellow,
provide a summer-long succession of
colour

The summer flowers of the Tulip Tree
are both unusual and attractive – from
the unfolding bud to the open bloom

Pruning This is usually carried out in early summer and consists of removing poorly placed shoots. In small gardens where space is limited trees may be pollarded (cut back to the crown) each year in spring. In this case 1.2–1.8m (4–6ft) of growth will be made annually.

Underplanting This is less satisfactory with Eucalyptus than with many other trees.

Pest and disease control These trees are not much troubled by pests, but they may be attacked by silver leaf disease. In this case remove and burn infected branches. Seedlings can be severely affected or even killed by damping off or *Botrytis cinerea,* grey mould. Control: use clean containers and composts, and treat seeds with thiram before sowing.

Propagation Usually by seeds sown indoors in early spring.

Season of interest	Winter	Spring	Late spring	Summer	Late summer	Autumn
In full leaf	X———	———	———	———	———	——X
Autumn colour				—		
Flowers				X—X		
Fruits						
Bark and stem	X———	———	———	———	———	——X

The following five characteristics determine to a great extent the amount of attention a specific tree requires.

	When planted	5 years	20 years
Height	450 mm	4·0 m	9·0 m
Width	150 mm	2·0 m	3·5 m
Root spread		3·0 m	5·0 m
Hardiness	C	C	C
Wind-firm		3	2/3

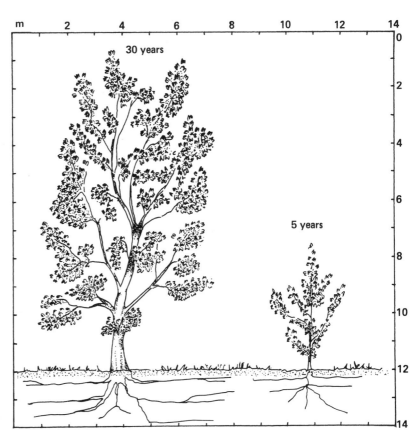

Plant care profile

	Minimum Average High
Site needs	X———X
Soil needs	X———X
Pruning	X———X
Staking	X———X
Maintenance	X———X

Fagus sylvatica – FAGACEAE
Beech, European Beech

Origin   Europe.
A hardy deciduous tree.

Uses
Beeches are possibly best used as specimen trees in gardens where space permits. The type is usually too large for most gardens, but the pendulous varieties are appreciably smaller. Hedging is another use of this subject.

Description
Dimensions   Old trees may eventually reach a size of 21–24m (70–80ft) high by 12–15m (40–50ft) wide.
Rate of growth   Usually slow in the early years, increasing to moderate and then slowing again later.
Life span   Variable, but trees over 70–100 years old begin to deteriorate.
Habit   A tree with a large, round-headed, spreading crown.
Leaves   Bright green in spring and summer, turning in autumn to shades of yellow, copper and brown. On young trees the leaves persist through winter.
Flowers   Insignificant.
Fruits   Brown husks covered with bristles when ripe.
Bark   Smooth, grey.

Features
The Beech is a majestic tree which makes a fine feature in most situations. It is hardy, wind-firm, requires little attention and is most pleasing to look at. The leaves cause few problems. Most varieties of Beech, although smaller than the species, are suitable for large gardens.
Pollution   Fairly tolerant.
Non-poisonous.

Varieties
Fagus sylvatica 'Aurea Pendula'. A form with a weeping habit and yellowish-green leaves.
Fagus sylvatica 'Dawyck'. A narrow columnar form, rarely more than 4–5m (13–17ft) wide.
Fagus sylvatica 'Pendula'. A weeping green Beech, makes a smaller tree, but is too large for small gardens.
Fagus sylvatica 'Purpurea Pendula'. A purple-leaved weeping variety.
Fagus sylvatica 'Zlatia'. Yellowish leaves.

Requirements
Position   Once it has become established Beech will grow in most situations and locations, including coastal, inland and some upland sites. This tree grows best in light shade when small, but prefers to be in the sun when large.
Soil   Most soils will support Beech, but avoid wet or heavy clay land. The finest trees are to be found on well drained chalk loams with a pH of 7–7.5.

Notes on culture

Planting Trees up to 4m (13ft) high can be successfully planted between autumn and spring, but autumn planting is preferable. Stake and tie until the roots take firm hold.

Space Allow a minimum 15m (50ft) diameter space at maturity, and 9m (30ft) from buildings.

Pruning Consists chiefly of forming the initial framework of branches. Subsequently only minimal pruning is needed, such as removing the odd crossing branch and cleaning up the stem as each tree grows.

Underplanting This is not particulary satisfactory with mature trees due to the usually dense leaf cover provided by Beech.

Pest and disease control Although there are a few troubles which affect Beech these are usually minor in nature, looking worse than they are. Aphids and greenfly, beech scale (insects covered in white, wool-like wefts) and weevils are the most common pests. A tar oil winter wash can work wonders for small trees but only spray when trees are dormant. Bracket fungi, canker, coral spot and honey fungus occasionally attack. In this case cut out affected parts and burn. Honey fungus can kill trees and may involve replanting. The long-term effects of Beech bark disease, a recent form of ailment, remain to be felt.

Propagation By seeds sown in autumn. Named varieties by grafting in spring.

Plant care profile

	Minimum	Average	High
Site needs		X	
Soil needs		X	
Pruning	X———X		
Staking		X	
Maintenance	X———X		

Season of interest	Winter	Spring	Late spring	Summer	Late summer	Autumn
In full leaf			X——————	———	—X	
Autumn colour	————	———	—X		X—	———
Flowers						
Fruits						
Bark and stem	———	———	—X			X—

The following five characteristics determine to a great extent the amount of attention a specific tree requires.

	When planted	5 years	20 years
Height	2·4 m	4·0 m	6·0 m
Width	900 mm	2·5 m	4·0 m
Root spread		3·5 m	5·0 m
Hardiness	A / B	A / B	A
Wind-firm		1 / 2	1 / 2

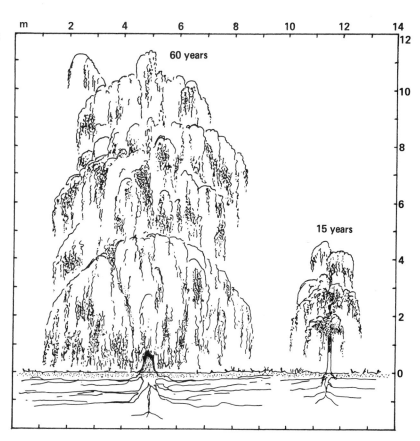

Fraxinus excelsior – OLEACEAE

Ash

Origin   Europe (including Britain) and Caucasus.
A very hardy deciduous tree.

Uses
The Ash, particularly in its weeping varieties, makes an effective specimen tree.

Description
Dimensions   Ultimate size rarely exceeds 7.5–9m (25–30ft) high by 3–4.5m (10–15ft) wide. However, where conditions are ideal the Ash can double or treble these measurements.
Rate of growth   Rapid in the early years, slowing to moderate with increasing maturity.
Life span   Trees mature at about 75 years, living for 200 years or more.
Habit   A fairly upright tree, rounded and spreading.
Leaves   Narrow pinnate leaves, medium green becoming pale yellowish-green in late summer.
Flowers   Greenish, appearing before the leaves open in mid-late spring.
Fruits   Green or brownish winged keys in clusters.
Bark   Light grey, becoming darker and furrowed with age.

Features
The Ash, though less colourful than many flowering trees, is an interesting tree throughout the year, partly by virtue of its summer leaves and partly the outline of the branches in winter with the black buds. The tree casts less shadow than many others. It is very hardy, wind-firm, and there is not much trouble from falling leaves. The lateness of leafing enables the frost-tender foliage to escape damage.
Pollution   A good tree for tolerating fumes and soot.
Non-poisonous.

Varieties
Fraxinus excelsior 'Aurea Pendula'. A weeping form with yellowish-green leaves.
Fraxinus excelsior 'Pendula'. A charming mushroom-shaped weeping tree, rather smaller than the type.

Requirements
Position   Although Ash can be grown in most parts of the temperate zone, better results are obtained if areas subject to late spring frosts and positions exposed to strong or cold winds are avoided. Given suitable soil conditions the Ash can be grown in coastal or inland districts, lowland and even highland areas. A sunny position is best, but light shade is tolerated.

Soil   Deep, moist, well drained loams that contain chalk or are neutral or slightly alkaline, pH 7–7.5, produce good specimens.

Notes on culture
Planting   Plant trees up to 4.5m (15ft) high between autumn and spring, making sure that the larger specimens are supported and tied until well established. Weeping varieties may need to have the leading shoot supported and lifted to ensure upward growth.
Space   Allow 5–6m (17–20ft) diameter space for the head when mature, and keep trees a minimum of 5m (17ft) away from buildings.
Pruning   Once the initial framework of branches has been formed the less cutting the better.

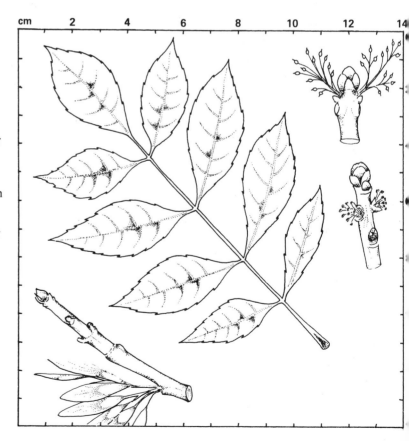

Underplanting   Although this tree is a gross feeder, shrubs and other garden plants can grow successfully beneath its branches, which cast only light shade.

Pest and disease control   Rarely a problem, but ash canker can cause a form of die-back. Cut out and burn affected parts.

Propagation   By seeds sown in autumn or spring. Named varieties by grafting in spring on seedling rootstocks.

Season of interest	Winter	Spring	Late spring	Summer	Late summer	Autumn
In full leaf			X———————————	———————————	———————————	—X
Autumn colour						
Flowers		X—X		—		
Fruits					X———	—X
Bark and stem	————————	—X				X-

The following five characteristics determine to a great extent the amount of attention a specific tree requires.

	When planted	5 years	20 years
Height	2·4 m	4·5 m	7·5 m
Width	1·0 m	2·5 m	3·5 m
Root spread		3·5 m	5·0 m
Hardiness	A/B	A/B	A
Wind-firm		1	1

Plant care profile

	Minimum Average High
Site needs	X
Soil needs	X
Pruning	X———X
Staking	X———X
Maintenance	X———X

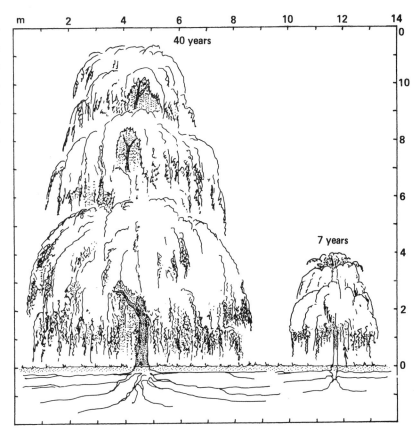

m 2 4 6 8 10 12 14

40 years

7 years

Gleditsia triacanthos – LEGUMINOSAE
Honey Locust, Three-thorned Acacia

Origin   North America.
A deciduous tree, hardy in the warm temperate zone.

Uses
The Honey Locust makes a good specimen tree or can be planted in shrubberies.

Description
Dimensions   Average ultimate size 6–9m (20–30ft) high by about 3.5–4.5m (12–15ft) wide.
Rate of growth   Varies from slow to moderate.
Life span   Trees of 80 years and over can be expected.
Habit   Rounded or upright.
Leaves   The foliage, which is pinnate, almost fern-like, is one of the main attractions. In autumn the leaves turn yellow.
Flowers   Greenish, appearing in clusters.
Fruits   In good years pinkish-brown seed pods, which later turn brown, appear in autumn and persist till spring, and often rattle in the wind.
Bark   Insignificant.

Features
The foliage of this tree is particularly attractive. As the alternative name suggests, the Three-thorned Acacia is well armed with sharp spines, which can be something of a nuisance. The tree is unfortunately only moderately hardy.
Pollution   Resistant.
Non-poisonous.

Varieties
Gleditsia triacanthos 'Bujoti'. A form with narrower leaflets and a pendulous habit.
Gleditsia triacanthos inermis.   A thornless form.
Gleditsia triacanthos 'Sunburst'. The leaves are a spectacular yellow as they unfold.

Requirements
Position   The Honey Locust can be grown without much difficulty in warm lowland sites. Sheltered situations in the sun or light shade, preferably with a south– or west-facing aspect, will suit best.
Soil   Ideally this should be a well drained but moist, fertile loam that is neutral or near-neutral, pH 7 or thereabouts, but this tree will tolerate some chalk.

Notes on culture
Planting   Can be carried out from autumn to spring, but use small plants not more than 2m (7ft) high as this tree resents being moved, especially when large. Tie young trees to canes until well rooted.
Space   Allow a space of about 4.5m (15ft) diameter for full grown specimens, and 3.5m (12ft) from buildings.
Pruning   This consists mainly of light trimming to shape and removing dead wood.

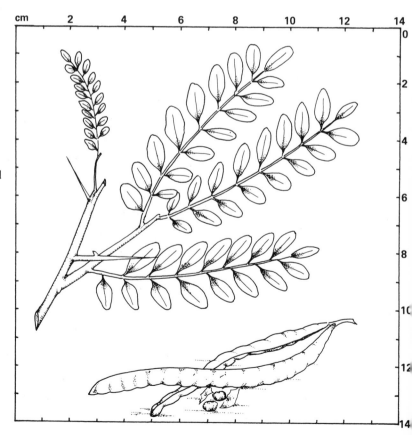

Underplanting   As only light shade is cast by the foliage, plants and shrubs may be planted below the branches without undue harm.
Pest and disease control   This tree is mostly trouble-free.
Propagation   By seeds sown outdoors in spring. Named varieties by layering in autumn, or grafting in spring under cover.

Season of interest	Winter	Spring	Late spring	Summer	Late summer	Autumn
In full leaf			X————		→X	
Autumn colour					X——→X	
Flowers						
Fruits	→X				X————	
Bark and stem						

The following five characteristics determine to a great extent the amount of attention a specific tree requires.

	When planted	5 years	20 years
Height	1·2 m	2·5 m	4·5 m
Width	450 mm	1·2 m	2·5 m
Root spread		2·0 m	3·5 m
Hardiness	C	C	C
Wind-firm		2/3	2

Plant care profile

	Minimum Average High
Site needs	X————X
Soil needs	X————X
Pruning	X————X
Staking	X————X
Maintenance	X————X

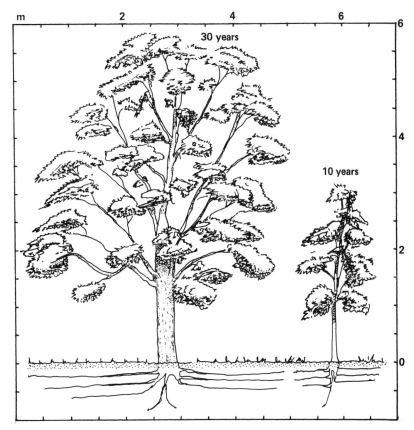

Koelreuteria paniculata
Golden Rain Tree

Origin   Northern China.
A moderately hardy deciduous tree.

Uses
With its unusual, almost star-like, arrangement of flowers,
K. paniculata makes a distinctive specimen tree and adds interest to a shrubbery.

Description
Dimensions   Average ultimate size 3–5m (10–17ft) high by 2.5–3m (8–10ft) wide.
Rate of growth   Slow to moderate.
Life span   Probably rarely exceeds 40–50 years.
Habit   A small, round-headed tree.
Leaves   Attractive foliage consisting of green pinnate leaves which develop yellow autumn tints.
Flowers   Small yellow flowers produced during summer in panicles up to 300mm (1ft) long.
Fruits   In hot summers the flowers are followed by greenish, hollow seed capsules tinged with red.
Bark   Brownish.

Features
The dainty foliage, the unusual yellow flowers, and the curious balloon-like seed capsules all serve to make this tree distinctive. This tree does not appear to have any bad traits, provided it is given the necessary conditions of shelter and warmth.
Pollution   Fairly tolerant.
Non-poisonous.

Varieties
Koelreuteria paniculata apiculata. A small, spreading tree.
Koelreuteria paniculata 'Fastigiata'. A narrower, more upright form.

Requirements
Position   Planting is necessarily confined to sheltered sites in warm temperate climates, and this tree is far more effective in colour and interest when grown in a warm, sunny, south-facing position that is free from late spring frosts and cold winds. Shelter from the north and east are necessary, as is a long growing season.
Soil   This tree is fairly easily satisfied as regards soil, but it will do best in slightly acid to neutral, well drained but moisture-retentive loam, with a pH range of 6.8–7.

Notes on culture
Planting   Small trees of 600–750mm (2–2½ft) can be moved more successfully than large specimens. They should be planted out between autumn and spring.
Space   Allow a space of 3m (10ft) diameter for headroom at maturity, and a minimum of 1.8m (6ft) from buildings.
Pruning   This chiefly consists of shaping the initial framework of branches. After that pruning is rarely necessary, apart from trimming the odd awkward shoot.
Underplanting   Low-growing shrubs, ground cover and bulbs grow well under the light foliage which casts only light shade as a rule.

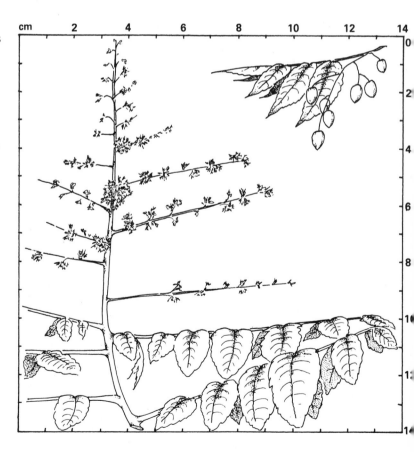

Pest and disease control Not usually necessary.

Propagation By seeds sown in autumn or spring; or root cuttings in heat in early spring. Root cuttings consist of pencil-thick pieces of root, about 50–75mm long, which are placed in pots or boxes of cutting compost and rooted under warm, moist conditions indoors.

Season of interest	Winter	Spring	Late spring	Summer	Late summer	Autumn
In full leaf			X———————X			
Autumn colour					X———X	
Flowers				X		
Fruits					X—X	
Bark and stem						

The following five characteristics determine to a great extent the amount of attention a specific tree requires.

	When planted	5 years	20 years
Height	1·2 m	2·5m	4·0m
Width	450mm	1·5m	2·5m
Root spread		2·5m	3·5m
Hardiness	C	C	C
Wind-firm		3	2

Plant care profile

	Minimum Average High
Site needs	X———X
Soil needs	X———X
Pruning	X———X
Staking	X
Maintenance	X

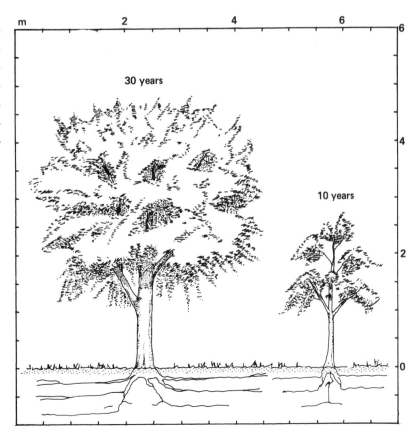

Laburnum anagyroides – LEGUMINOSAE
Common Laburnum

Origin Central and Southern Europe.
A hardy deciduous tree.

Uses
Laburnums can be used as specimen trees, in groups and in shrubberies.

Description
Dimensions Average ultimate size 4.5–7.5m (15–25ft) high by 2.5–4m (8–13ft) wide.
Rate of growth Variable from slow to moderate, decreasing with age.
Life span Laburnums generally speaking are not long-lived and can start to decline after about 35 years.
Habit Variable, ranging from rounded to upright and pendulous forms.
Leaves A dull green, which becomes yellowish as leaf fall approaches.
Flowers Hanging racemes of yellow flowers which provide colour in spring and summer, making this one of the most showy of trees.
Fruits Green pendulous pods, turning brownish when ripe.
Bark Greenish-grey.

Features
The colourful, conspicuous flowers are the main attraction of the Laburnum. The tree is hardy and wind-firm, and it is root-firm in most conditions, except on wet, heavy, clay land. A disadvantage is that most parts of the tree are poisonous, especially the seeds, which should be kept away from young children.
Pollution Resistant.
Poisonous.

Varieties
Laburnum anagyroides 'Aureum'. Golden-yellowish leaves.
Laburnum anagyroides 'Autumnale'. A variety which frequently carries a second flower crop in autumn.
Laburnum anagyroides 'Erect'. An upright form, narrower than the type.
Laburnum anagyroides 'Pendulum'. A weeping form.
Laburnum x *watereri*. A variety with very long flower racemes and glossy leaves.
Laburnum x *watereri vossii*. Similar to *L.* x *watereri* but without glossy leaves.

Requirements
Position Laburnums, being quite frost-hardy, can be successfully grown in most lowland parts of the cool temperate zone. They grow and flower well in coastal areas or inland, in full sun or light shade. Shelter from cold or strong winds is desirable, however.
Soil The best and longest-lived specimens are usually found on well drained loams that are slightly acid, having a pH of about 6.5, but the Laburnum will also grow in neutral soil.

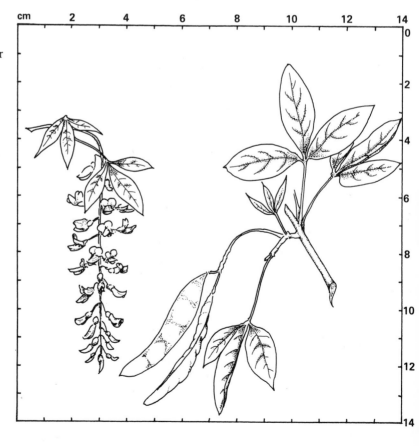

Notes on culture

Planting Trees up to 2.5–3m (8–10ft) high should be planted between autumn and spring. Support trees with stakes and ties until they become established.

Space The roots of this tree are less damaging to the foundations of buildings than many. However, avoid placing trees nearer than 3m (10ft) from stem to structures and allow a space of 4m (13ft) diameter at maturity.

Pruning Consists of shaping the initial crown framework. After the head is formed further pruning becomes unnecessary.

Underplanting Laburnums only cast light shade which allows many plants and bulbs to grow successfully beneath branches.

Pest and disease control Leaf miner, which causes leaf disfiguration, is more unsightly than serious and can be checked by spraying with diazinon. Semi-circular holes in leaves are usually the work of leaf-cutter bees. They are not serious and often hardly noticeable. Silver leaf disease can attack Laburnum. Cut out affected areas or fell and burn badly diseased trees.

Propagation By seeds sown in autumn in a cold frame, and planted out the following year. Named varieties by grafting on seedling stocks in spring.

Plant care profile

	Minimum Average High
Site needs	X
Soil needs	X——X
Pruning	X——X
Staking	X——X
Maintenance	X——X

Season of interest	Winter	Spring	Late spring	Summer	Late summer	Autumn
In full leaf			X———	———	————	—X
Autumn colour						
Flowers			X——X			
Fruits						
Bark and stem						

The following five characteristics determine to a great extent the amount of attention a specific tree requires.

	When planted	5 years	20 years
Height	2·1 m	3·5 m	6·0 m
Width	750 mm	2·0 m	3·5 m
Root spread		3·0 m	4·5 m
Hardiness	A/B	A	A
Wind-firm		3	2/3

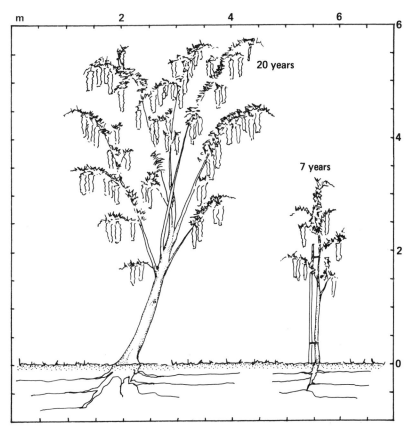

Liquidambar styraciflua – ALTINGIACEAE
Sweet Gum

Origin   North America.
A moderately hardy deciduous tree.

Uses

The Sweet Gums may be used as specimen trees or among shrubs, but the main aim should be to position them so that the autumn colouring is seen to maximum advantage.

Description

Dimensions   Average size at maturity 5–7.5m (17–25ft) high by 2.5–3.5m (8–12ft) wide.
Rate of growth   Moderate in early years, decreasing with age.
Life span   In mild temperate areas there are specimens of 70 years and more that will probably survive for some years yet.
Habit   Usually pyramidal.
Leaves   Palmate, downy and sweetly fragrant, dark green in summer turning vivid orange and crimson shades in autumn. The young leaves are frost-tender.
Flowers   Insignificant, arranged in rounded group.
Fruits   Brownish clusters.
Bark   The corky bark of mature trees is quite striking in winter.

Features

The main attraction of the Sweet Gum is the foliage which is pleasantly fragrant, and provides fine autumn tints in vivid shades of orange and crimson. The leaves, which resemble those of maple, are carried singly and not in pairs, providing a useful means of identification.
Pollution   Moderately tolerant.
Non-poisonous.

Variety

Liquidambar styraciflua 'Aurea'. Yellowish-green leaves.

Requirements

Position   The Sweet Gum needs a sunny, sheltered, lowland site in a mild or warm area. It should be given protection from wind and late spring frosts, and if possible a south- or west-facing aspect. Sites in light shade are tolerated in sunny areas, but trees in sunny positions produce the best autumn colours.
Soil   This tree flourishes on well drained loam or moist, deep sandy soils that are neutral, with a pH around 7. Avoid overfeeding or the autumn colours will be less intense.

Notes on culture

Planting   Trees up to 3m (10ft) high can be moved between autumn and spring, but make sure the fleshy roots are intact and undamaged. Stake and tie trees until they are well established.
Space   Allow an area of 4m (13ft) diameter and the same distance from buildings.
Pruning   This consists of forming and shaping a good framework of branches. As the trees grow and mature it will only be necessary to remove crossing and surplus branches.

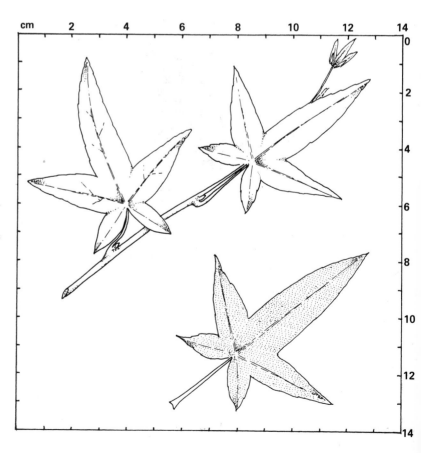

Underplanting Low-growing ground cover plants, such as dwarf types of Berberis and Hypericum grow satisfactorily below its branches.
Pest and disease control Rarely necessary.
Propagation By seeds sown in autumn. Named varieties by layering in spring.

Season of interest	Winter	Spring	Late spring	Summer	Late summer	Autumn
In full leaf			X———————————X			
Autumn colour					X———X	
Flowers						
Fruits						
Bark and stem						

The following five characteristics determine to a great extent the amount of attention a specific tree requires.

	When planted	5 years	20 years
Height	1·8m	2·5m	4·5m
Width	750mm	1·2m	3·0m
Root spread		2·0m	4·0m
Hardiness	C	B/C	B/C
Wind-firm		2	1/2

Plant care profile

	Minimum	Average	High
Site needs		X———X	
Soil needs		X———X	
Pruning	X———X		
Staking		X	
Maintenance		X———X	

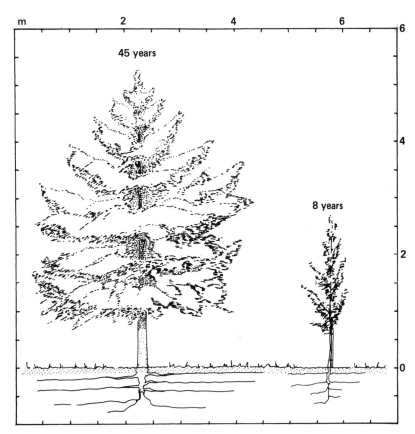

Liriodendron tulipifera – MAGNOLIACEAE
Tulip Tree

Origin Eastern North America.
A hardy deciduous tree.

Uses
The Tulip Tree makes a good specimen tree on lawns. The type is more suited to the large garden than the small, but some of the varieties take up less space.

Description
Dimensions Although in its native forests the Tulip Tree can grow to well over 30m (100ft) high, in cooler climates its ultimate size rarely exceeds 6–9m (20–30ft) high by 3–4.5m (10–15ft) wide.
Rate of growth In early years can be rapid, up to 600mm (2ft) or more per year, but slows down with age.
Life span In excess of 100 years.
Habit Broadly rounded or upright.
Leaves Unusually-shaped leaves, yellowish-green in spring, turning first yellow and then brown in autumn.
Flowers Quite attractive, yellowish-green with a touch of orange near the centre, produced in summer.
Fruits Cone-shaped and insignificant.
Bark Dark greyish-brown.

Features
The autumn leaf colouring is the outstanding feature of this tree. The leaves are unusually shaped, and the flowers, though attractive and produced in abundance on mature trees, are not outstandingly conspicuous. The only disadvantage of the Tulip Tree is that its foliage can be damaged by late spring frosts.
Pollution Fairly tolerant.
Non-poisonous.

Varieties
The following varieties take up less space than the type:
Liriodendron tulipifera 'Aureomarginatum'. Leaves margined with yellow.
Liriodendron tulipifera 'Fastigiatum'. An erect tree.

Requirements
Position Given the right conditions this tree can be grown in most lowland parts of the mild temperate zone. The ideal situation is a well sheltered site protected from north and east winds. A south-facing position in full sun or with light shade for part of the day will help to ensure good autumn colouring.

Soil The Tulip Tree thrives on well drained, deep, rich loams that are slightly acid to neutral, having a pH around 6.3–7.

Notes on culture
Planting Trees, up to 2m (7ft) high, should be planted between autumn and spring. Stake and tie until established. Smaller trees can be moved more easily and grow more rapidly than larger ones. Trees over 900mm (3ft) high should preferably be container-grown stock.
Space Allow an area of 6m (20ft) diameter and at least the same distance from buildings.

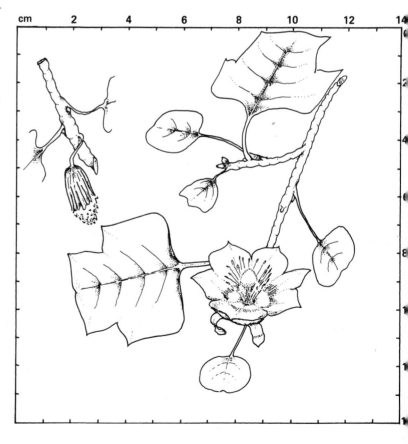

Pruning The only pruning that is usually necessary is trimming, or shortening straggling shoots in late autumn or winter, or removing surplus growths to form a framework of well-spaced branches.
Underplanting The vigorous nature of the tree, and its use as a specimen do not make it practical to plant beneath the Tulip Tree.
Pest and disease control These trees seem to be quite trouble-free.
Propagation By seeds sown in autumn; or layering in spring.

Season of interest	Winter	Spring	Late spring	Summer	Late summer	Autumn
In full leaf			X———————X			
Autumn colour					X———X	
Flowers				X		
Fruits						X
Bark and stem						

The following five characteristics determine to a great extent the amount of attention a specific tree requires.

	When planted	5 years	20 years
Height	900mm	3·5m	7·5m
Width	300mm	1·5m	3·5m
Root spread		2·5m	5·0m
Hardiness	B/C	B	B
Wind-firm		1/2	1

Plant care profile

	Minimum Average High
Site needs	X
Soil needs	X
Pruning	X———X
Staking	X———X
Maintenance	X———X

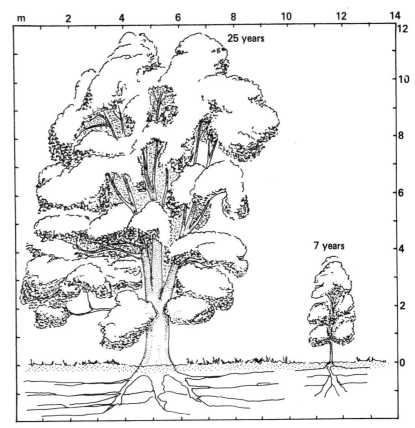

Malus hupehensis – ROSACEAE
Crab, Hupeh Crabapple

Origin　China and Japan.
A hardy deciduous tree.

Uses
The fruits can be cooked, but
M. hupehensis is primarily
decorative. It may be planted singly
as a specimen or in a shrubbery, or
if space allows in a group of two or
more.

Description
Dimensions　Average ultimate size
7.5–9m (25–30ft) high by 4.5–6m
(15–20ft) wide.
Rate of growth　Fairly rapid during
the first few years, slowing to
moderate after eight or ten years.
Life span　Not yet well established,
the tree being of fairly recent
introduction, but seems likely to be
50 years and over.
Habit　Rounded or upright with
stiffly ascending branches.
Leaves　Bright green, darkening in
summer, yellowing with dull
crimson tints in autumn.
Flowers　Fragrant, tinged with pink
in bud, opening white, produced in
abundance in late spring.
Fruits　Red-tinted yellow
crabapples appearing in late
summer and autumn.
Bark　Greyish, becoming darker
and rough surfaced with maturity.

Features
The appeal of this tree rests on its
blossom and fruit. It has no bad
traits and has the advantages of
being hardy and wind-firm.
Pollution　Fairly tolerant.
Non-poisonous.

Variety
Malus hupehensis　'Rosea'. A
pink-flowered form.

Requirements
Position　This flowering Crab can
be grown successfully in most
lowland parts of the temperate
zone. Its needs as regards site are
modest. An open, sunny situation,
either inland or in a coastal district,
will suit *M. hupehensis,* provided it
is sheltered from north and east
winds, especially at flowering time.
Soil　This tree will do best in a
deep, well drained soil, containing
some chalk but neutral in reaction,
with a pH of about 7.

Notes on culture
Planting　Trees up to 4m (13ft)
can safely be moved between
autumn and spring. Provide support
and tie until firmly rooted.
Space　Allow 6m (20ft) diameter
space for development and at least
4.5m (15ft) from buildings.
Pruning　Prune when young to
form a well shaped crown;
thereafter only to cut out diseased
or crossing branches. When
building up the initial framework
remove shoots with a narrow
crotch.
Underplanting　A wide range of
low-growing shrubs, ground cover
plants and bulbs can be successfully
grown beneath the branches of this
crabapple.

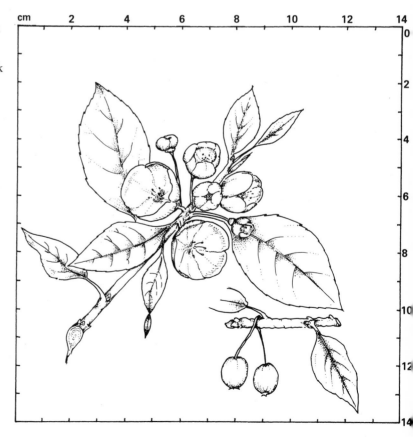

Pest and disease control The same problems which affect apples in the fruit garden also trouble crabapples. The most usual are: caterpillars, which eat the foliage; apple mildew disease, attacking leaves, fruits and shoots; and scab, mainly disfiguring foliage and fruits. All can be controlled by spraying, with fenitrothion against caterpillars, benomyl for mildew and scab.

Propagation By grafting in spring or budding in summer on apple rootstocks. Malling II or seedling stocks are preferred. The type can be raised from seed, but this takes several years more to reach flowering size than grafting or budding.

Season of interest	Winter	Spring	Late spring	Summer	Late summer	Autumn
In full leaf			X—————		—→X	
Autumn colour					X———	—→X
Flowers						
Fruits						
Bark and stem						

The following five characteristics determine to a great extent the amount of attention a specific tree requires.

	When planted	5 years	20 years
Height	2·4 m	4·0 m	7·5 m
Width	1·2 m	2·5 m	5·0 m
Root spread		3·5 m	6·0 m
Hardiness	A/B	A	A
Wind-firm		1/2	1

Plant care profile

	Minimum	Average	High
Site needs		X	
Soil needs		X	
Pruning		X	
Staking		X	
Maintenance		X	

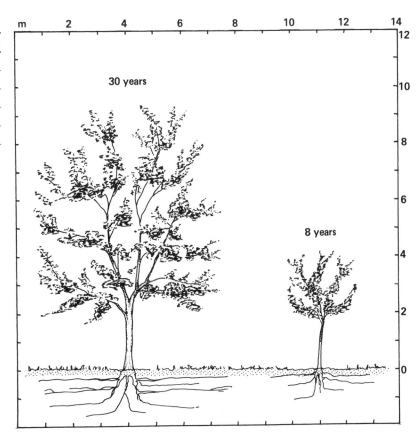

30 years

8 years

Malus x purpurea – ROSACEAE
Purple Crab

Origin A hybrid between *Malus niedzwetzkyana* and *Malus floribunda atrosanguinea*.
A hardy deciduous hybrid tree.

Uses
The Purple Crab may be planted in more formal gardens. It is very effective as a single specimen on a lawn, among shrubs, or in a group of two or more in gardens, open spaces or amenity areas.

Description
Dimensions Average ultimate size 6–7.5m (20–25ft) high by 3–5m (10–17ft) wide.
Rate of growth Fairly fast initially, slowing down later.
Life span Trees start to decline after 30–40 years.
Habit The Purple Crab has a more open branch framework than the Hupeh Crab.
Leaves The pointed leaves, which open a delicate mauve-purple in spring, then become a more intense purple-maroon, remaining that colour until leaf fall.
Flowers Ruby-red buds, opening out into shades of purple, produced in late spring.
Fruits Purple-tinted crabapples, appearing in late summer and autumn.
Bark Dark grey.

Features
The Purple Crab is outstanding for the purple colouring which appears in leaves, flowers and fruit. The tree is wind-firm and is an example of a good garden type.
Pollution Fairly tolerant.
Non-poisonous.

Varieties
There are one or two varieties, including *Malus* x *purpurea* 'Pendula', a weeping form, but the type *M.* x *purpurea* is hard to beat.

Requirements
Position A cool or mild temperate lowland site suits this tree well. It needs an open, sunny, south-facing situation and shelter from the north and east.
Soil A deep well drained loam that is moist and slightly acid, pH 6.5, is best, but a neutral soil is also satisfactory. This tree seems to have a tendency to mildew in dry ground conditions.

Notes on culture
Planting Trees up to 3m (10ft) high can safely be moved between autumn and spring. Stake, tie and keep supported until established.
Space Allow 5m (17ft) diameter space for development and a minimum of 3m (10ft) from buildings.
Pruning This is usually carried out in winter and consists of developing a main framework of branches in young trees. No further pruning should be necessary, except for cutting out any dead, diseased or crossing branches.

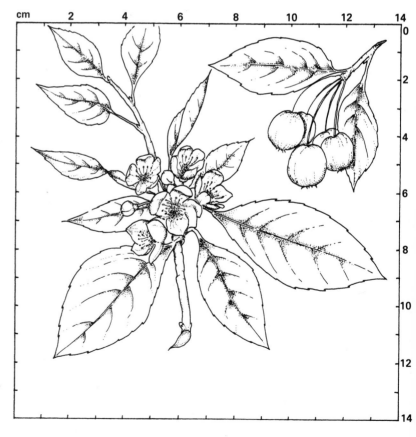

Underplanting Ground-cover plants and bulbs can be effectively used under this tree.
Pest and disease control As for *M. hupehensis*.
Propagation Usually by grafting in spring or budding in summer on selected rootstocks, such as Malling II.

Season of interest	Winter	Spring	Late spring	Summer	Late summer	Autumn
In full leaf			X—————		————	X
Autumn colour						X—X
Flowers			X			
Fruits					X—X	
Bark and stem						

The following five characteristics determine to a great extent the amount of attention a specific tree requires.

	When planted	5 years	20 years
Height	2·4 m	3·8 m	4·5 m
Width	1·2 m	1·5 m	3·5 m
Root spread		3·0 m	4·5 m
Hardiness	B	A/B	A/B
Wind-firm		1/2	1

Plant care profile

	Minimum	Average	High
Site needs		X	
Soil needs		X	
Pruning		X	
Staking		X	
Maintenance		X	

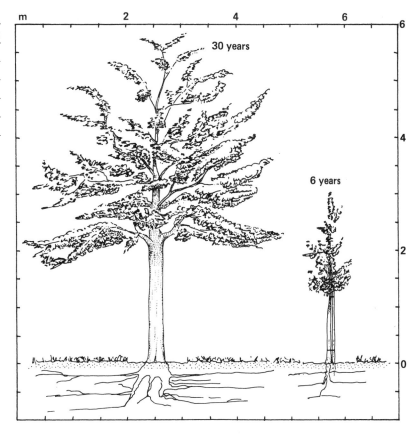

Malus tschonoskii – ROSEACEAE
Crab, Tschonosk Crabapple

Origin Japan.
A hardy deciduous tree.

Uses
This tree is excellent used as a single specimen or among shrubs. It can also be effectively used as an avenue tree in residential developments or open spaces. Being fairly resistant to pollution it is especially useful for town planting.

Description
Dimensions Average ultimate size 9–12m (30–40ft) high by 3–4m (10–13ft) wide.
Rate of growth Moderate.
Life span Probably the same as that of other Crabs – about 40–50 years or more.
Habit A pyramidal tree with fairly stiff ascending branches.
Leaves Bright green on opening, becoming darker in summer, turning to various shades of crimson, red, yellow and orange in autumn.
Flowers Whitish, usually appearing in late spring.
Fruits A Dull red, flushed with yellow, produced in late summer. Unfortunately they drop fairly quickly.
Bark Dark grey.

Features
The main attraction of this tree is the autumn leaf colour, and it can be depended on to colour well in most years. This Crab is hardy and wind-firm. The flowers and fruits give added interest.
Pollution Resistant.
Non-poisonous.

Varieties
At present there are no noteworthy varieties of this species. There does however appear to be considerable variation among stocks available, some are much more prolific in their flowering and fruiting than others. When buying trees of this variety obtain them if possible from a supplier with a floriferous strain or selection.

Requirements
Position This Crab can be planted in sheltered sites in most lowland parts of the cool temperate zone. Protection from either cold or freezing spring winds is necessary. A sunny site is preferable, but *M. tschonoskii* will tolerate some light shade for part of the day. As this tree is resistant to pollution a town site is suitable.
Soil A deep, well drained sandy loam, preferably well supplied with potash, and just slightly acid, pH about 6.5, will serve admirably. Neutral soil is also satisfactory. The autumn colouring can be less intense in high rainfall areas, especially where soil drainage is poor or trees are overfed.

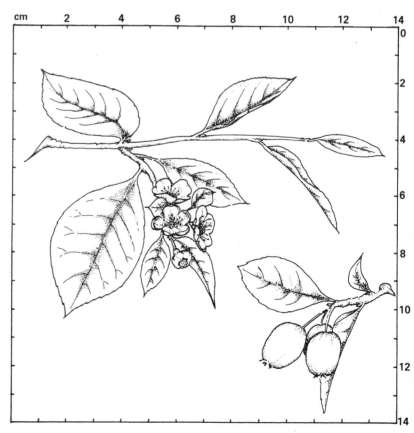

Notes on culture

Planting Trees up to 3–4m (10–13ft) can safely be planted between autumn and spring. Support, stake and tie trees of all sizes until root-firm.

Space Allow 4m (13ft) diameter space for development and the same distance from buildings.

Pruning This mainly involves regulating the number and spacing of shoots in the formative stage. In later years remove dead, diseased or crossing branches and trim as necessary to keep in shape.

Underplanting Ground cover plants and bulbs look attractive beneath this tree.

Pest and disease control Caterpillars and mildew may cause problems. Spray as necessary, with fenitrothion for caterpillars, benomyl for mildew and scab.

Propagation By grafting in spring or budding in summer on seedling rootstocks or selected rootstocks such as Malling II.

Season of interest	Winter	Spring	Late spring	Summer	Late summer	Autumn
In full leaf			X————————		—X	
Autumn colour					X———	—X
Flowers			X			
Fruits					X	
Bark and stem						

The following five characteristics determine to a great extent the amount of attention a specific tree requires.

	When planted	5 years	20 years
Height	2·4 m	3·5 m	6·0 m
Width	900 mm	1·2 m	2·0 m
Root spread		2·0 m	3·0 m
Hardiness	A	A	A
Wind-firm		1/2	1

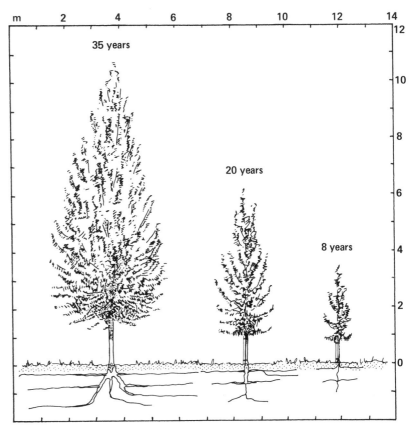

Plant care profile

	Minimum Average High
Site needs	X
Soil needs	X
Pruning	X
Staking	X
Maintenance	X———————X

Morus nigra – MORACEAE
Black Mulberry

Origin   Western Asia, China and North America.
A moderately hardy deciduous tree.

Uses
The main use is as a specimen tree, usually in association with buildings. The fruits of the Mulberry are also highly valued by some.

Description
Dimensions   Sizes vary, but some of 200 years old are no more than 4.5–6m (15–20ft) high by 3–4.5m (10–15ft) wide.
Rate of growth   Slow, in some cases very slow.
Life span   The Mulberry is long-lived and there are several which are believed to be at least 300 years old.
Habit   A small, squat, round-headed tree with a fairly dense crown.
Leaves   Usually heart-shaped, and green, without spectacular autumn tints.
Flowers   Cylindrical and lacking colour.
Fruits   Sweet dark red or black fruits, produced in late summer.
Bark   Dark grey-brown.

Features
The chief attractions are the sturdy picturesqueness and fruits. The Mulberry is wind-firm and has no bad habits. Its chief drawback perhaps is its slow growth rate.
Pollution   Fairly tolerant.
Non-poisonous.

Varieties
There are no outstanding variations of the type at present.

Requirements
The Mulberry grows best in a warm or mild climate; elsewhere its cultivation is likely to be unsatisfactory. It needs a warm and sheltered site, protected from cold winds and late spring frosts. A sunny, south-facing aspect is preferable, but in the warmer parts of the temperate zone a west-facing aspect, shaded for part of the day only, will meet its basic needs.
Soil   Rich, deep, fertile loams that are well drained and almost neutral, pH 6.8, are ideal.

Notes on culture
Planting   Mulberries are usually planted between autumn and spring. Smaller trees move with less disturbance than large, but as the Mulberry is so slow-growing the largest trees that can be obtained commercially, about 1.8–2m (6–7ft) provide a compromise. Stake and tie until established.
Space   Allow a 3m (10ft) diameter space for growth, which the planter is unlikely to witness. In favourable situations also allow at least 4.5m (15ft) from buildings. However, two-thirds of this figure should be adequate in cooler areas.

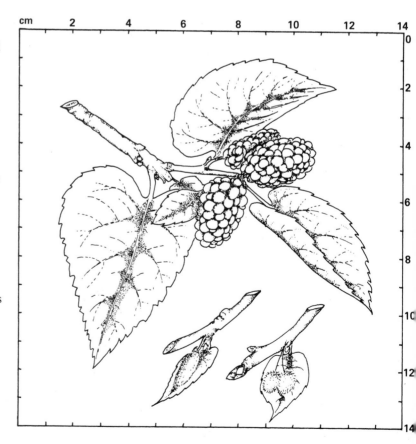

Pruning Avoid cutting this tree any more than is absolutely necessary. Any essential pruning is best carried out in winter, to keep bleeding to a minimum.
Underplanting Evergreen ground cover plants in subdued colours are satisfactory.
Pest and disease control Mulberries are virtually untouched by pests. However, canker and die-back occasionally damage *M. nigra.* In this case cut out and burn affected parts.
Propagation By cuttings of two-year-old wood, taken in autumn and semi-ripe cuttings in summer.

Season of interest	Winter	Spring	Late spring	Summer	Late summer	Autumn
In full leaf			X————	————	————	—X
Autumn colour						
Flowers			X—X			
Fruits					X—X	
Bark and stem						

The following five characteristics determine to a great extent the amount of attention a specific tree requires.

	When planted	5 years	20 years
Height	1·2 m	1·8 m	3·0 m
Width	600 mm	750 mm	1·0 m
Root spread		1·5 m	2·0 m
Hardiness	C	B/C	B/C
Wind-firm		1/2	1

Plant care profile

	Minimum	Average	High
Site needs		X——X	
Soil needs		X——X	
Pruning	X		
Staking		X	
Maintenance	X——X		

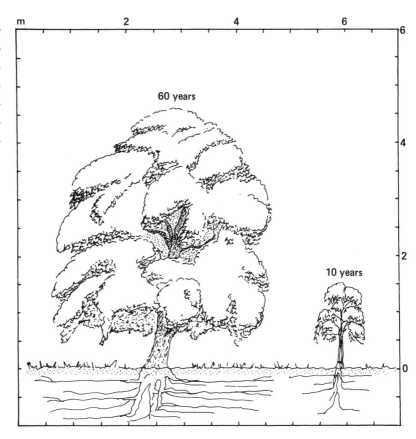

60 years

10 years

95

Parrotia persica – HAMAMELIDACEAE
Parrot's Tree

Origin   Caucasus and Iran.
A moderately hardy deciduous tree.

Uses
P. persica, a member of the Witch Hazel family, has not been widely planted but it deserves to be better known. It excels as a specimen, decorative tree.

Description
Dimensions   Average ultimate size 3–5m (10–17ft) high by 3–4m (10–13ft) wide.
Rate of growth   Slow.
Life span   Trees of 50 years and over have been noted.
Habit   A small, broadly rounded tree, spreading with age.
Leaves   Mid-green, turning in autumn to crimson and gold shades.
Flowers   Individually insignificant, but the stamens are usually plentiful and give the tree a reddish glow in spring.
Fruits   Brown, nut-like and inconspicuous.
Bark   Flakes off the main stem after the style of Plane trees, giving a variegated effect. The removal of some of the lower branches enables this to be seen to advantage.

Features
The main feature of this tree is the fine autumn leaf colour. The bark also provides added interest.
Pollution   Fairly tolerant.
Non-poisonous.

Varieties
There do not appear to be any readily available varieties of this tree, but as there is some variation among seedlings, some producing less colourful autumn effects than others, increase by layering from good colouring types is recommended.

Requirements
Position   This tree needs a sunny, sheltered site in the mild or warm temperate zone. A south-facing aspect suits it well.
Soil   The ideal, to judge from a few fine specimens, appears to be a well drained sandy loam just on the acid side of neutral, pH 6.5.

Notes on culture
Planting   Small trees, up to 2m (7ft) high, may be planted between autumn and spring, but early planting while the soil is still warm is best. Stake and tie until well established.
Space   Allow a minimum 5m (17ft) diameter space for development at maturity and at least 3m (10ft) from buildings.
Pruning   This consists mainly of regulating the initial framework of branches. Little or no pruning is required later.

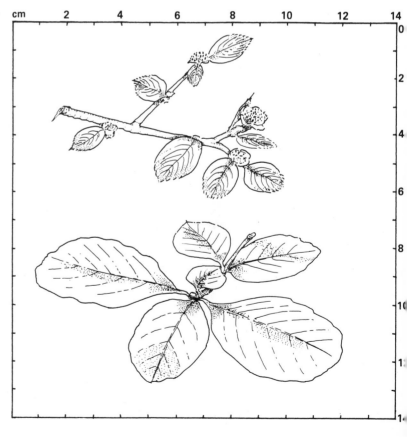

Underplanting This tree is probably seen to maximum advantage without any underplanting of shrubs, which would conceal part of the bark. *Pest and disease control* This tree appears to be trouble-free. *Propagation* Can be by seeds sown in autumn, which could possibly result in some new variation. However, layers taken in late summer or early autumn are quicker, and good colour from good trees can be assured.

Season of interest	Winter	Spring	Late spring	Summer	Late summer	Autumn
In full leaf			X————		—X	
Autumn colour					X—X	
Flowers		X—X				
Fruits						
Bark and stem	X———————————————————————————X					

The following five characteristics determine to a great extent the amount of attention a specific tree requires.

	When planted	5 years	20 years
Height	1·2 m	2·0 m	4·0 m
Width	450 mm	1·5 m	3·0 m
Root spread		2·5 m	4·0 m
Hardiness	C	B/C	B/C
Wind-firm		1/2	1

Plant care profile

	Minimum Average High
Site needs	X———X
Soil needs	X———X
Pruning	X———X
Staking	X———X
Maintenance	X

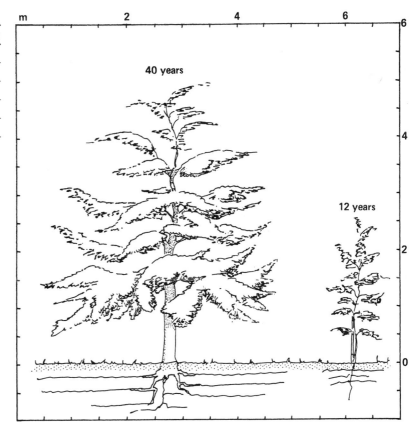

40 years

12 years

Paulownia tomentosa – SCROPHULARIACEAE
Paulownia or Anna's Tree

Origin China.
A deciduous tree hardy in warm, temperate climates.

Uses
Paulownias make useful specimen trees when planted alone in grass and they are also effective singly or as a group among shrubs.

Description
Dimensions Average ultimate size 4.5–7.5m (15–25ft) high by 3–4.5m (10–15ft) wide.
Rate of growth Moderate to rapid, according to method of treatment.
Life span Variable, but 40 years is not uncommon.
Habit This tree naturally forms a rounded crown, but when it is pruned hard the growth is more upright and the leaves are much larger.
Leaves A feature of this tree. Green and broadly heart-shaped, they vary from 120–250mm (5–10in.) to over 600mm (2ft) long. Not outstanding for autumn colour.
Flowers The flower buds form at the tips of shoots in autumn and open in spring to show lavender blue petals. However, except in mild districts and coastal areas the flower buds are liable to be damaged in winter.
Fruits Ovoid capsules, but set and develop rather infrequently.
Bark Brownish-grey.

Features
The large green leaves are excellent for creating tropical effects, especially when cut back each spring. The flowers can be very attractive, where the climate allows them to escape the frost. The trees are usually wind-firm.
Pollution Moderately tolerant.
Non-poisonous.

Variety
Paulownia fargesii. Closely resembles *P. tomentosa* but flowers slightly later in summer and grows slightly larger. This is now called P. lilacina.

Requirements
Position Planting should be confined to lowland districts of the warm temperate zone. Coastal districts are often suitable. The best results are obtained in sheltered but sunny sites, preferably having a south or south-west aspect.
Soil This should be well drained, ideally a deep, fertile loam that is about neutral, pH 7. When planting on thin, gravelly land, dig a larger-than-usual tree pit and fill with prepared soil.

Notes on culture
Planting Small rather than large trees can be planted from autumn to spring, preferably in autumn while the soil is still warm. If necessary prepare larger tree pits for planting. Stake and tie until trees are firmly rooted.
Space Allow individual specimens 4.5m (15ft) diameter space. Trees in groups can be planted 2.5 (8ft) apart. In either case allow a minimum of 3m (10ft) from buildings.

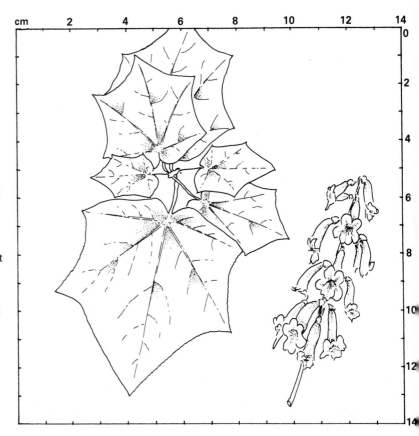

Pruning This consists initially of forming a framework of branches, which can be treated subsequently in one of two ways. In the warmest areas the cutting is kept to a minimum to encourage flowering. In the cooler areas the young growths can be removed close to the main stems and branches each spring. This treatment, together with watering and feeding, will promote vigorous growth, up to 1.8m (6ft) and over per year, together with larger leaves.

Underplanting Bulbs are suitable.

Pest and disease control The Paulownia is rarely troubled by pests, but honey fungus and leaf-spot occasionally appear. Check leaf-spot by spraying with a copper fungicide, and dig out dead tree stumps to remove the source of honey fungus infection.

Propagation Most commonly by seeds, usually imported from European countries, sown in spring. May also be propagated by cuttings in summer or by root cuttings in spring. Root cuttings consist of pencil-thick pieces of root, about 50-75mm (2–3in.), which are placed in containers of cutting compost, and rooted under cover in warmth.

Season of interest	Winter	Spring	Late spring	Summer	Late summer	Autumn
In full leaf			X———————————————X			
Autumn colour						
Flowers			X—X			
Fruits						
Bark and stem						

The following five characteristics determine to a great extent the amount of attention a specific tree requires.

	When planted	5 years	20 years
Height	1·2 m	3·0 m	5·0 m
Width	600 mm	2·0 m	3·5 m
Root spread		3·0 m	4·5 m
Hardiness	C	C	C
Wind-firm		2	1/2

Plant care profile

	Minimum Average High
Site needs	X———X
Soil needs	X———X
Pruning	X———X
Staking	X———X
Maintenance	X———X

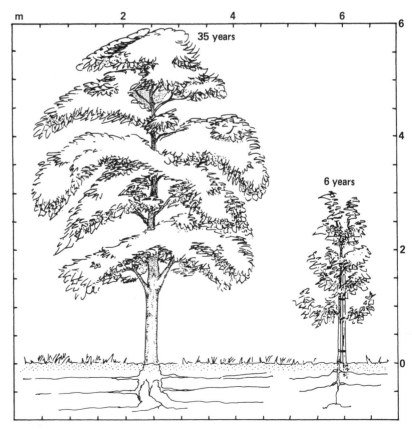

Populus alba – SALICACEAE
White Poplar

Origin   Eastern and Southern Europe, Western Asia and Western Siberia.
A hardy deciduous tree.

Uses
The White Poplar is useful as a specimen tree, in a group of two or more, or when used as a screen in large-scale planting.

Description
Dimensions   Average ultimate size 9–12m (30–40ft) high by 4.5–7.5m (15–25ft) wide.
Rate of growth   Rapid for the first few years, moderate later.
Life span   Trees often go into decline after 30 years or so.
Habit   An upright tree. Some stocks of Poplar are inclined to send up suckers or shoots.
Leaves   In spring and summer the leaves are grey-green on the upper surface and white and felt-like on the underside. The general effect is of white foliage. In autumn this becomes yellow and crimson.
Flowers   Grey catkins in spring.
Fruits   Whitish catkins with seeds protected by hairs.
Bark   The bark of trunks and stems is relatively insignificant, but the tips of young shoots are white and woolly at first.

Features
The main attraction without doubt is the foliage, both the white of foliage and tips of shoots in spring and summer, followed by the autumn colour. The tree is hardy and wind-firm, and although some suckering may occur this can be controlled.
Pollution   Fairly tolerant.
Non-poisonous.

Varieties
Populus alba   'Pyramidalis'. A narrow pyramidal tree.
Populus alba   'Richardii'. Leaves golden on the upper surface and woolly below.

Requirements
Position   The White Poplar may be planted in coastal or inland districts. A sunny, moist, cool sheltered position in a mild or temperate zone site that is not subject to dry freezing winds is most suitable. Hot, dry situations appear less favourable to this tree.
Soil   A cool, deep, well drained but moist neutral loam, pH 7, will suit best.

Notes on culture
Planting   Trees up to 2.5–3m (8–10ft) should be planted from autumn to spring. Stake and tie until firmly rooted.
Space   Allow a minimum of 6m (20ft) diameter space for development and at least the same distance from buildings. On clay or heavy soils avoid planting closer to buildings than 9m (30ft), to prevent undue drying out of the land and possible sinkage of foundations.
Pruning   This consists mainly of cutting out badly placed or diseased shoots during the formative stage. Later treatment is negligible, just removing poorly placed or diseased branches and suckers, if any.

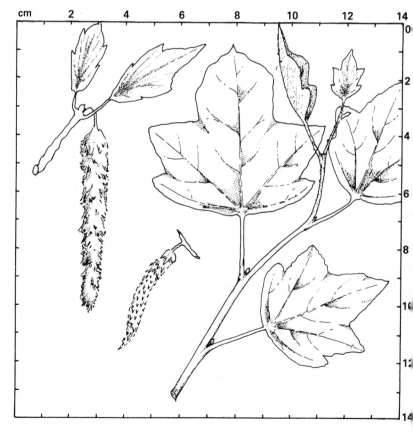

Underplanting This practice is not particularly satisfactory, especially where the trees are furnished with foliage to ground level.

Pest and disease control The main pests are aphids or greenfly, caterpillars and poplar beetle. Control by spraying with derris or malathion for aphids and greenfly, derris or fenitrothion for caterpillars, HCH dust is one means of control for the poplar beetle. Diseases which sometimes cause problems are: canker, which affects stems and branches; bracket fungi, which usually start on dead wood; die-back, which also affects stems and branches; leaf-spot fungi and rust, both of which affect leaves; and silver leaf. Spray with a copper fungicide for leaf-spot and with thiram for rust. Cut out and burn affected parts in the case of bracket fungi, canker, die-back or silver leaf.

Propagation Usually by cuttings taken in summer or autumn. Suckers can be used but are obviously more likely to give trouble from suckering than trees raised from cuttings.

Plant care profile

	Minimum	Average	High
Site needs		X	
Soil needs		X	
Pruning		X	
Staking	X——X		
Maintenance		X	

Season of interest	Winter	Spring	Late spring	Summer	Late summer	Autumn
In full leaf			X————		—X	
Autumn colour					X——	—X
Flowers		X				
Fruits						
Bark and stem						

The following five characteristics determine to a great extent the amount of attention a specific tree requires.

	When planted	5 years	20 years
Height	2·4 m	4·5 m	7·5 m
Width	600 mm	2·5 m	4·0 m
Root spread		3·5 m	5·0 m
Hardiness	B	A/B	A/B
Wind-firm		2	1/2

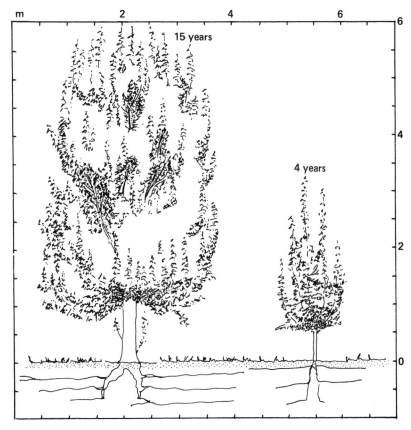

Prunus avium – ROSACEAE

Gean, Wild Cherry, Mazzard

Origin   Europe (including Britain) and Western Asia.
A deciduous tree, hardy in most temperate areas.

Uses

P. avium and its varieties may be planted as specimen trees on lawns or in shrubberies. The double variety in particular makes an outstanding specimen tree.

Description

Dimensions   Average ultimate size 9–12m (30–40ft) high by 6–9m (20–30ft) wide. But on good land trees can exceed these dimensions.
Rate of growth   Rapid at first, becoming moderate with age.
Life span   Trees start to decline after about 50 years.
Habit   Variable from broadly pyramidal to pendulous.
Leaves   Green in summer, turning crimson in autumn in warm, dry years.
Flowers   White, either single or double, appearing in profusion in spring.
Fruits   Round, dark or blackish red.
Bark   Shiny, peeling horizontally.

Features

The blossom is the main attraction, but the bark, fruits and autumn leaves have considerable appeal.
P. avium is wind-firm and reliable, blooming every year provided the tree is healthy. This Cherry is one of the parents of the cultivated fruiting sorts.
Pollution   Tolerant.
Non-poisonous.

Varieties

Prunus avium 'Decumana'. Notable for its large, single flowers and long leaves.
Prunus avium 'Pendula'. A stiffly pendulous form.
Prunus avium 'Plena'. Outstanding for its masses of long-lasting double flowers.

Requirements

Position   These trees can be successfully grown in most parts of the temperate zone. They flower most abundantly and produce the best autumn colouring in open and sunny but sheltered sites in mild areas. Situations that are lightly shaded for part of the day can be suitable also.
Soil   A well drained neutral or chalky loam with a pH of about 7 suits well.

Notes on culture

Planting   Trees up to 2.5–3m (8–10ft) high may be planted between autumn and early spring. Avoid excessively deep planting on badly drained soil or weak, stunted growth can result. Stake and tie all plants over 600mm (2ft) until firmly rooted.
Space   Allow 9m (30ft) diameter space for development and 6m (20ft) from buildings.
Pruning   The tree should be pruned when young to form a basic framework of suitably spaced branches. Subsequent treatment involves the minimum of cutting, nothing more than the removal of crossing branches and any dead or diseased wood. This should be carried out in late summer ideally.

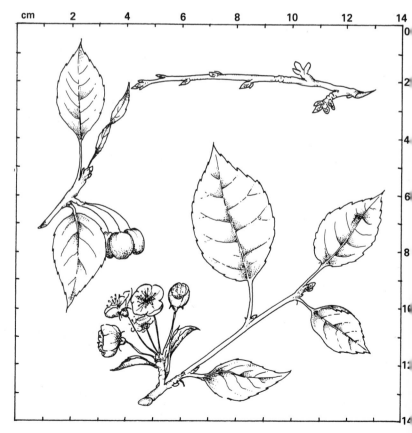

Underplanting Low growing shrubs, ground-cover plants and bulbs can be effectively used beneath the branches of P. avium and varieties.

Pest and disease control The main pests of the Wild Cherry are aphids and caterpillars, which can be checked by malathion and fenitrothion sprays respectively. The principal diseases and disorders are bacterial canker, chlorosis, honey fungus and silver leaf, which can be troublesome individually or collectively. Cut out parts affected by canker or silver leaf; spray with iron sequestrene to overcome chlorosis; dig out dead tree stumps to remove sources of honey fungus infection; saw down and burn trees that are badly affected by silver leaf.

Propagation By seeds sown in autumn. Named varieties by budding in late summer.

Season of interest	Winter	Spring	Late spring	Summer	Late summer	Autumn
In full leaf			X————	—————	—X	
Autumn colour					X———	—X
Flowers		X—X				
Fruits						
Bark and stem	X————	————	————	————	————	—X

The following five characteristics determine to a great extent the amount of attention a specific tree requires.

	When planted	5 years	20 years
Height	2·4 m	4·5 m	7·5 m
Width	750 mm	3·5 m	6·0 m
Root spread		4·5 m	7·0 m
Hardiness	A/B	A	A
Wind-firm		1	1

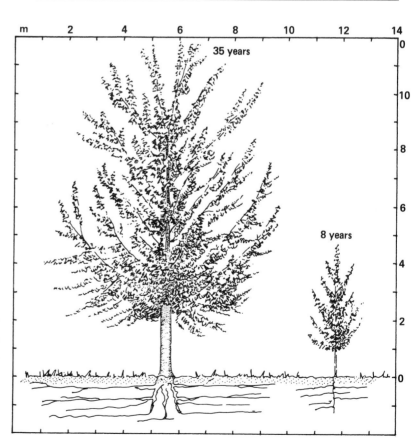

Plant care profile

	Minimum Average High
Site needs	X
Soil needs	X
Pruning	X———X
Staking	X———X
Maintenance	X

Prunus cerasifera – ROSACEAE
Cherry Plum, Myrobalan Plum

Origin Believed to be Balkans and Caucasus.
A hardy deciduous tree.

Uses
The standard green-leaved Cherry Plum is quite often planted in milder districts to form a screen or windbreak, or even an impenetrable hedge. The dark-leaved forms are very useful as specimen trees on lawns or planted in shrubberies.

Description
Dimensions Average ultimate size 6–7.5m (20–25ft) high by 4.5–7.5m (15–25ft) wide.
Rate of growth Rapid initially, becoming moderate or slow after a few years.
Life span Trees start to decline after about 40–50 years.
Habit A round-headed tree.
Leaves Green in summer, turning yellowish or dull wine in autumn.
Flowers White flowers appearing in early spring.
Fruits Red and yellow cherry-shaped plums in summer and autumn.
Bark Greyish, insignificant.

Features
The blossom, though white, is even more effective than the red and yellow fruits. This tree is normally wind-firm and can stand up quite well to cool winds.
Pollution Resistant.
Non-poisonous.

Varieties
Prunus cerasifera 'Nigra'. Pinkish flowers which later turn almost white. Deep purple to black leaves.
Prunus cerasifera 'Pendula'. A compact small tree of pendulous habit.
Prunus cerasifera 'Pissardii'. (Purple-leaved Plum). Attractive crimson-purple foliage.

Requirements
Position There are few districts in the cool temperate zone where the Cherry Plum and its varieties cannot be grown, and the coloured-leaf varieties can put on a brave show of foliage colour in quite an exposed position or in partial shade. However, where flowers and fruit are the main consideration a warm, well sheltered, sunny situation in a mild temperate climate is most suitable.
Soil A well drained loam, preferably neutral, pH 7, should give good results.

Notes on culture
Planting Trees up to 3m (10ft) high may be planted between autumn and spring, but planting is best completed by the onset of winter. All trees need staking and tying until settled into their new site.
Space Allow single specimen trees 7.5m (25ft) diameter space for development. When planted as a windbreak the trees should be quite close, 3–4m (10–13ft) apart or even closer. In either case plant no closer to buildings than 4.5m (15ft).

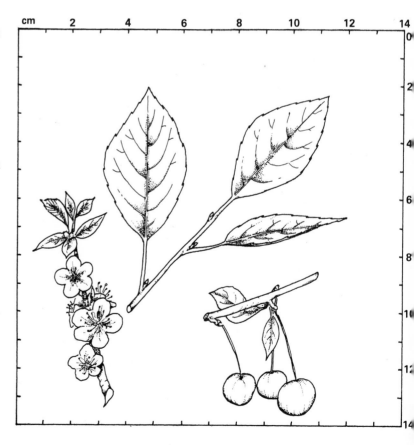

Pruning This mainly consists of encouraging the formation of a crown of well spaced and suitably placed branches. Subsequent treatment involves keeping the crown in shape by occasional trimming and the removal of any diseased or crossing branches.

Underplanting Bulbs are perhaps the most suitable for this purpose.

Pest and disease control As for *P. avium*.

Propagation By seeds sown in autumn. Named varieties and those with coloured foliage by budding in summer on seedling or other stocks or by layering in spring.

Season of interest	Winter	Spring	Late spring	Summer	Late summer	Autumn
In full leaf			X⟵	⟶	⟶X	
Autumn colour					X—X	
Flowers		X—	—X			
Fruits					X—X	
Bark and stem						

The following five characteristics determine to a great extent the amount of attention a specific tree requires.

	When planted	5 years	20 years
Height	2·4 m	3·5 m	5·0 m
Width	750 mm	3·5 m	5·0 m
Root spread		4·5 m	6·0 m
Hardiness	A	A	A
Wind-firm		1	1

Plant care profile

	Minimum	Average	High
Site needs	X—	—X	
Soil needs		X	
Pruning	X—	—X	
Staking	X—	—X	
Maintenance		X	

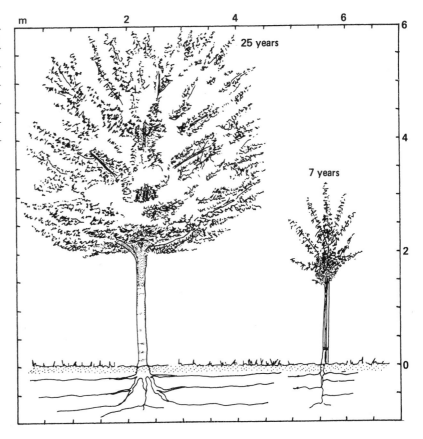

Prunus dulcis – ROSACEAE

Common Almond

Origin   North Africa to Western
Asia.
A moderately hardy deciduous tree.

Uses

The Almond is excellent as a
specimen tree in grass, planted
against a wall or among shrubs.

Description

Dimensions   Average ultimate size
5–7.5m (17–25ft) high by a similar
width, but in cool sites may reach
little more than half this height or
width.
Rate of growth   Rapid in early
years, moderate later.
Life span   Trees over 50 years old
are getting past their best.
Habit   Upright initially, spreading
with age to form a more rounded
crown.
Leaves   Lanceolate green leaves
which in some hot, dry years turn
dull crimson just before leaf fall,
but colouring is not a regular
feature.
Flowers   Pink flowers which
appear before the leaves in spring.
Fruits   In warm, sunny areas with
well drained soil a crop of nuts may
be produced in autumn.
Bark   Grey-brown and
inconspicuous.

Features

The Almond is seen to its greatest
advantage in spring when the bare
branches are smothered in flowers.
The tree is wind-firm and
frost-hardy in winter, but the
flowers are easily damaged by
spring frosts or cold winds.
Pollution   Tolerant.
Non-poisonous.

Varieties

Prunus dulcis   'Alba'. Single white
flowers.
Prunus dulcis   'Macrocarpa'. Pale
pink flowers and the best nuts.
Prunus dulcis   'Roseoplena'.
Double rose-pink flowers.

Requirements

Position   The cultivation of the
Almond is for the most part
confined to lowland areas in the
mild or warm temperate zones and
in exposed sites to a position
against a south wall. Choose a
south or south-west aspect for
preference.
Soil   Ideally this should be a deep,
well drained medium loam, neutral
or chalky, with a pH of about
7–7.2.

Notes on culture

Planting   Trees up to 3m (10ft)
tall can be planted from autumn to
spring, but preferably in autumn.
Stake and tie all trees until
established. Those trained against a
wall will need a framework of
horizontal wires or similar.
Space   In mild climates the
Almond requires a space of about
7.5m (25ft) diameter at maturity.
Allow about 4.5m (15ft) where
planted and grown against a wall or
building.
Pruning   This consists of regulating
the development of the crown
framework of branches either as a
rounded head or fan-trained against
a wall.

Underplanting Low, ground-cover plants and bulbs can be effectively used under P. dulcis and varieties.
Pest and disease control Aphids and various caterpillars can be troublesome at times, but can be checked by malathion and fenitrothion sprays respectively. The most common diseases are bacterial canker, peach leaf curl, silver leaf and chlorosis. Spray in autumn, early and mid-spring with benomyl or a copper fungicide to control peach leaf curl and use iron sequestrene for chlorosis as necessary. Cut out and burn parts infected by canker or silver leaf.
Propagation By seeds sown in autumn. Named varieties by budding in summer onto seedling or other stocks.

Season of interest	Winter	Spring	Late spring	Summer	Late summer	Autumn
In full leaf			X	────		X
Autumn colour						X
Flowers		X──X				
Fruits					X	
Bark and stem						

The following five characteristics determine to a great extent the amount of attention a specific tree requires.

	When planted	5 years	20 years
Height	2·4 m	4·0 m	4·5 m
Width	600 mm	3·0 m	4·0 m
Root spread		4·0 m	5·0 m
Hardiness	C	B/C	B/C
Wind-firm		2	1/2

Plant care profile

	Minimum Average High
Site needs	X──X
Soil needs	X──X
Pruning	X
Staking	X
Maintenance	X──X

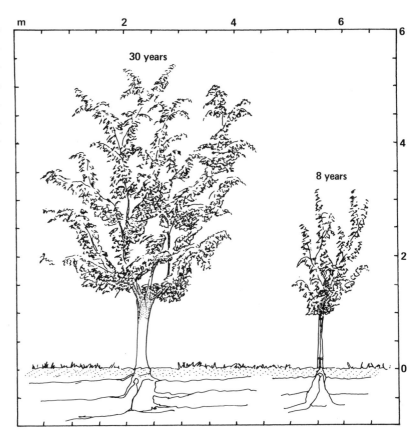

30 years

8 years

107

Prunus padus – ROSACEAE
Bird Cherry

Origin   Europe (including Britain) and Asia.
A very hardy deciduous tree.

Uses
The Bird Cherry makes a good specimen tree as well as being suitable for planting in shrubberies. As *P. padus* occurs naturally in some places it may be possible to relate the planting of garden varieties to the wild type.

Description
Dimensions   Average ultimate size 6–9m (20–30ft) high by 4.5–6m (15–20ft) wide.
Rate of growth   Moderate to rapid.
Life span   This tree is longer-lived than many of the Cherries, having a life span of some 60–70 years or more.
Habit   Trees are fairly open and upright in the earlier years, filling out and becoming more spreading later.
Leaves   Green, oval with pointed tip.
Flowers   White, slightly fragrant, produced in racemes during spring.
Fruits   Black, bitter, but popular with birds, hence the common name of the tree.
Bark   Dark grey.

Features
The flower spikes are the main attraction, but the dark green leaves can provide a useful background for colourful summer flowering plants. The Bird Cherry is usually well rooted and wind-firm. The bark and young shoots when bruised have an unpleasant, acrid smell.
Pollution   Fairly tolerant.
Non-poisonous.

Varieties
Prunus padus 'Albertii'. Strong and erect in habit, flowers profusely.
Prunus padus commutata   A very early flowering variety, two to three weeks earlier than the type.

Prunus padus 'Watereri'. The longest flower-spikes of any Bird Cherry.

Requirements
Position   As the Bird Cherry is very hardy and later flowering than some Cherries it can be planted in most lowland areas of the cool or mild temperate zone. An open site, preferably sunny or lightly shaded for only part of the day, is suitable. However, it is advisable for the final position to have a south- or west-facing aspect and to be protected from cold north and east winds.

Soil   Provided that the ground is well drained, not excessively heavy or sandy and at least 300–450mm (12–18in.) deep, this tree should grow satisfactorily. The Bird Cherry thrives in neutral soil but will also tolerate slightly acid conditions, growing well in land with a pH of 6–7.

Notes on culture
Planting   Trees up to 3m (10ft) should be planted between autumn and spring. After planting, tying and staking is needed, especially in more open situations, until trees are firmly rooted.
Space   Allow 6m (20ft) diameter space for development and a further 4.5m (15ft) from buildings.

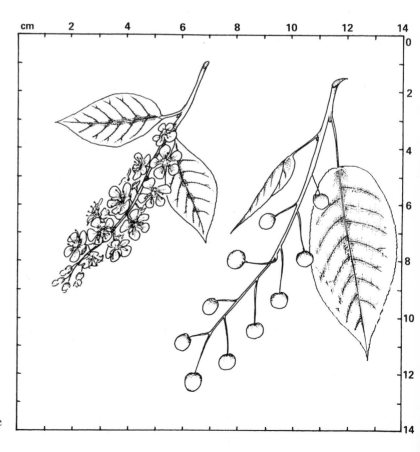

Pruning   This mainly consists of forming the initial framework. Subsequent pruning requirements are minimal.

Underplanting   This tree may be underplanted with shrubs or low ground cover as it does not cast a dense shade.

Pest and disease control   As for *P. avium.*

Propagation   By stratified seed sown in spring. Named varieties by budding on seedling or other rootstocks in summer.

Season of interest	Winter	Spring	Late spring	Summer	Late summer	Autumn
In full leaf			X————————————————→X			
Autumn colour						
Flowers			X			
Fruits						
Bark and stem						

The following five characteristics determine to a great extent the amount of attention a specific tree requires.

	When planted	5 years	20 years
Height	2·4 m	4·0 m	5·0 m
Width	600 mm	3·0 m	4·0 m
Root spread		4·0 m	5·0 m
Hardiness	B	B	B
Wind-firm		1/2	1

Plant care profile

	Minimum	Average	High
Site needs		X	
Soil needs		X	
Pruning	X————X		
Staking	X————X		
Maintenance	X————X		

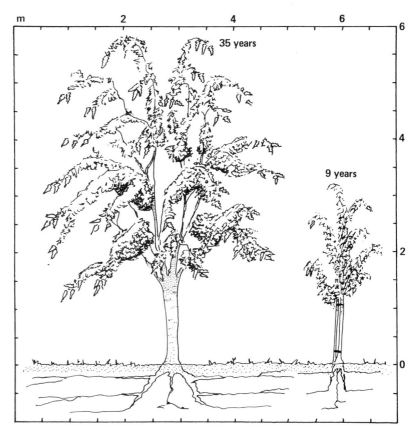

Prunus persica – ROSACEAE
Common Peach

Origin China.
A moderately hardy deciduous tree.

Uses
There are a number of excellent varieties of Peach, weeping and otherwise, which can be good as specimens in grass, when planted in shrubberies, or against a wall.

Description
Dimensions Average ultimate size 4.5–7.5m (15–25ft) high by about the same wide.
Rate of growth Rapid in early years, becoming moderate with age.
Life span Can be quite short, with trees going into decline after 30 years.
Habit A broadly rounded tree.
Leaves Narrowly lanceolate, and dark green.
Flowers Single pink, appearing in early spring before the leaves open.
Fruits Yellow, tinged pink or crimson, plum-like with downy skin.
Bark Dark or brownish-grey.

Features
The blossom is the chief attraction of this tree, but unfortunately the flowers can be easily damaged by frost. The leaves are not particularly outstanding, but they do not hide the fruits unduly.
Pollution Tolerant.
Non-poisonous.

Varieties
The Peach has long been cultivated and there are available several very good varieties which extend the colour range of the flowers. The true type or species is rarely planted now.
Prunus persica 'Alboplena'. Long-lasting, white double flowers.
Prunus persica 'Alboplena Pendula'. A weeping form with white double flowers.
Prunus persica 'Foliis Rubis'. Purplish-red young leaves.
Prunus persica 'Klara Mayer'. A fine form with pink double flowers.

Prunus persica 'Prince Charming'. An upright form with rose-red double flowers.
Prunus persica 'Russell's Red'. Crimson double flowers.
Prunus persica 'Windle Weeping'. A weeping form with broad leaves and double pink flowers.

Requirements
Position The ornamental Peach is hardy only in the warm or mild parts of the temperate zone and planting it in cool districts is a bit of a gamble. Ideally the site should be in full sun, south-facing, protected from late spring frosts and cold north or east winds. Trees planted in cooler districts need the protection of a wall with either a south or a westerly aspect.

Soil This should be warm, well drained and slightly acid, with a pH around 6.5. If the soil is too alkaline chlorosis may occur.

Notes on culture
Planting Trees up of 1.8–2.5m (6–8ft) high can be planted from autumn to spring. However it is best to plant in autumn while the soil is still warm. Stake and tie all trees after planting, supporting them until well established.
Space Allow trees on good soils in warm districts a space of 7.5m (25ft) diameter. Trees planted against walls in cooler areas will need a minimum 4.5 (15ft) of wall space.

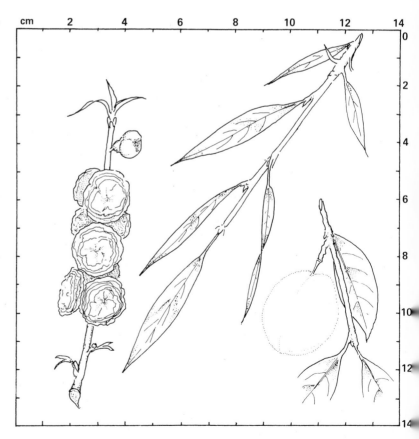

Pruning This mainly consists of the initial shaping of the framework of branches into either a bushy head or a fan-shaped wall form. Wall-trained forms require careful pruning throughout their lives. Very little subsequent treatment is necessary for other trees, it is simply a matter of removing straggling shoots as necessary to maintain shape.

Underplanting Shrubs, ground cover plants and bulbs can be grown successfully in the light shade cast by this tree.

Pest and disease control Aphids and caterpillars are occasionally troublesome but can be kept in check with fenitrothion sprays. The major problem with these trees is without doubt peach leaf curl disease. This can be checked by a copper or other fungicide, which will need to be applied at least three times, once during the autumn, again during early spring and once more 28 days later.

Propagation By seed sown in autumn. Named varieties by budding on common plum rootstocks.

Season of interest	Winter	Spring	Late spring	Summer	Late summer	Autumn
In full leaf			X—		—→	X
Autumn colour						
Flowers		X				
Fruits					X—X	
Bark and stem						

The following five characteristics determine to a great extent the amount of attention a specific tree requires.

	When planted	5 years	20 years
Height	1·8 m	4·0 m	5·0 m
Width	450 mm	3·0 m	4·0 m
Root spread		4·0 m	5·0 m
Hardiness	C	C	B/C
Wind-firm		2	1/2

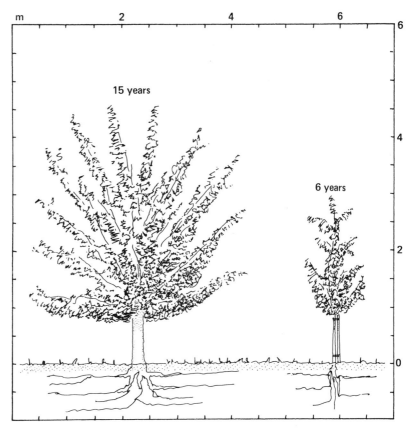

Plant care profile

	Minimum Average High
Site needs	X——X
Soil needs	X
Pruning	X
Staking	X
Maintenance	X

Prunus serrulata – ROSACEAE
Japanese Cherry

Origin   China and Korea.
A hardy deciduous tree.

Uses
These ornamental Cherries are almost impossible to beat for floral beauty and make ideal specimen trees on lawns, in shrubberies, in open spaces and in residential areas.

Description
Dimensions   Average ultimate size 6–7.5m (20–25ft) high and 6–7.5m (20–25ft) wide.
Rate of growth   Rapid to moderate, depending on variety and conditions.
Life span   Variable from about 30 to 70 years.
Habit   Variable, but most varieties of this group of Japanese Cherries are flat-topped and with a spreading habit.
Leaves   Vary from mid-green to reddish or brown-tinged, some turning yellowish or crimson shades in autumn.
Flowers   Typically double or semi-double, ranging through many shades of white, pink and rose, the majority appearing in early or late spring.
Fruits   Small black cherry.
Bark   Quite attractive, tending to split and peel horizontally.

Features
The outstanding attraction is the masses of blossom which appear in late spring. One characteristic of this tree, is its habit of forming a flat top, with the ascending branches keeping the foliage clear of the main stem, exposing the horizontally peeling bark.
Pollution   Resistant.
Non-poisonous.

Varieties
It would be impossible to list in this short space all the worthwhile varieties of Japanese Cherry, but here is a selection of the more popular members of the group.

Prunus serrulata 'Fudanzakura'. A small, round-headed form with pinkish-white single flowers from autumn to spring.
Prunus serrulata 'Kanzan'. A profusion of large, pink double flowers.
Prunus serrulata 'Kiku-shidare Sakura' (Cheal's Weeping Cherry). A small tree with drooping branches, deep pink double flowers.
Prunus serrulata 'Shirofugen'. Pink buds opening double white, bronze young foliage. Late.
The true species is now mainly represented in cultivation by the Japanese flowering varieties.

Requirements
Position   The Japanese Cherries can be grown in most parts of the mild temperate zone. They grow best and flower most profusely in open, sunny positions, but will tolerate light shade for part of the day. Those varieties which flower in winter and early spring should be protected from northerly and easterly freezing winds.
Soils   The soil must be well drained and should ideally be a deep, sandy loam just on the acid side of neutral, with a pH of around 6.6–6.8.

Notes on culture

Planting Trees up to 3m (10ft) high should be planted from autumn to spring. Stake and tie all trees after planting, supporting them until well rooted.

Space Allow a minimum of 9m (30ft) diameter space for development and a further 5m (17ft) from buildings.

Pruning Requirements are modest, and consist mainly of shaping the initial framework, removing or shortening surplus branches. Subsequently no pruning should be necessary beyond the cutting out of crossing, straggling or diseased branches. Prune in late summer.

Underplanting This tree and its varieties can be effectively underplanted with spring-flowering bulbs.

Pest and disease control As for P. avium.

Propagation Most garden-worthy Japanese Cherries are named varieties and are increased by budding on seedling or selected stocks in summer.

Season of interest	Winter	Spring	Late spring	Summer	Late summer	Autumn
In full leaf			X————	————	—X	
Autumn colour					X——	—X
Flowers		X———	—X			
Fruits						
Bark and stem	X————	————	————	————	————	—X

The following five characteristics determine to a great extent the amount of attention a specific tree requires.

	When planted	5 years	20 years
Height	2·4 m	4·0 m	6·0 m
Width	750 mm	2·5 m	5·0 m
Root spread		3·5 m	6·0 m
Hardiness	B	B	B
Wind-firm		1/2	1

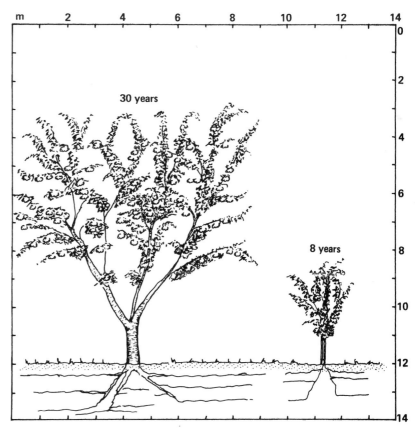

Plant care profile

	Minimum	Average	High
Site needs		X———X	
Soil needs		X	
Pruning	X———X		
Staking	X———X		
Maintenance	X———X		

113

Prunus subhirtella – ROSACEAE
Spring Cherry, Oshima Cherry

Origin Japan.
A hardy deciduous tree.

Uses
P. subhirtella and varieties may be used as specimen trees or planted in shrubberies. *P.s.* 'Autumnalis', the Autumn Cherry, in particular, can make an excellent specimen tree close to the house, providing colour and interest during the dark days of winter.

Description
Dimensions Average ultimate size 6–9m (20–30ft) high by 4.5–7.5m (15–25ft) wide.
Rate of growth Moderate to rapid.
Life span Not well established, but trees of 35 years and more look well.
Habit Variable, but trees are usually broadly rounded.
Leaves Green, broadly oval with point, and serrated leaf margins.
Flowers The type flowers during spring before the leaves appear, and its winter-flowering varieties bloom intermittently between autumn and spring. The predominant flower colours are shades of pink or pinkish-white.
Fruits Black cherry, but occurs only on rare occasions.
Bark Brown with lighter-coloured, horizontal markings.

Features
The main attraction of this tree is the appearance of delicate, pale pink flowers among the leafless branches in autumn, winter and early spring.
Pollution Fairly tolerant.
Non-poisonous.

Varieties
Prunus subhirtella ascendens A form with a tall, erect habit, producing pink or white flowers in early spring.
Prunus subhirtella 'Autumnalis' (Autumn Cherry). A form which blooms from autumn to spring. The flowers are white and semi-double.

Prunus subhirtella 'Autumnalis Rosea'. Similar to *P.s.* 'Autumnalis' but with pink flowers.
Prunus subhirtella 'Fukubana'. Bright pink, semi-double flowers.
Prunus subhirtella 'Pendula'. A weeping form, smaller than the type, with arching branches covered in spring with small, pink blossoms.
Prunus subhirtella 'Pendula Plena Rosea'. Rose-pink, semi-double flowers.
Prunus subhirtella 'Pendula Rubra'. Deep rose flowers and darker foliage.

Requirements
Position The Spring and Autumn Cherries can be grown and will flower in sheltered lowland sites throughout the mild temperate zone, but the best results will be obtained in warmer districts. They need shelter from cold winds and should preferably be given a position with a south or south-west aspect, in full sun but protected from the north and east.
Soil This should be a light or medium loam that is well drained and nearly neutral, pH around 6.8, also grows in slightly alkaline conditions above 7.

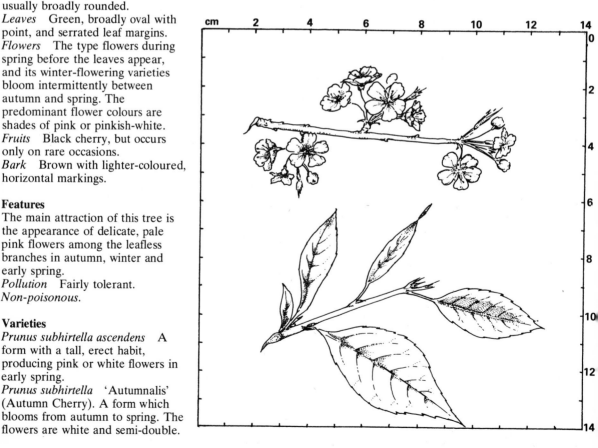

Notes on culture

Planting Trees up to 3m (10ft) high should be planted between autumn and spring. Stake and tie all trees after planting. Weeping or pendulous varieties may require additional support until the desired stem height is achieved.

Space An area of about 7.5m (25ft) diameter is needed for mature trees, and while advantage may be taken of the shelter provided by buildings it is unwise to plant closer to them than about 5m (17ft).

Pruning This consists of regulating the growth and development of the crown, after which very little cutting is necessary.

Underplanting Shrubs, ground cover plants and bulbs can be effectively used under P. subhirtella.

Pest and disease control As for P. avium.

Propagation Named varieties by cuttings taken in summer; or budding on rootstocks, also in summer.

Season of interest	Winter	Spring	Late spring	Summer	Late summer	Autumn
In full leaf			X———	———	———	——X
Autumn colour						
Flowers	————	———X			X——	—
Fruits						
Bark and stem	X———	———	———	———	———	——X

The following five characteristics determine to a great extent the amount of attention a specific tree requires.

	When planted	5 years	20 years
Height	2·4 m	3·8 m	6·5 m
Width	750 mm	3·0 m	4·5 m
Root spread		4·0 m	5·5 m
Hardiness	C	B/C	B/C
Wind-firm		1/2	1

Plant care profile

	Minimum	Average	High
Site needs		X———	—X
Soil needs		X	
Pruning	X———	—X	
Staking	X———	—X	
Maintenance	X———	—X	

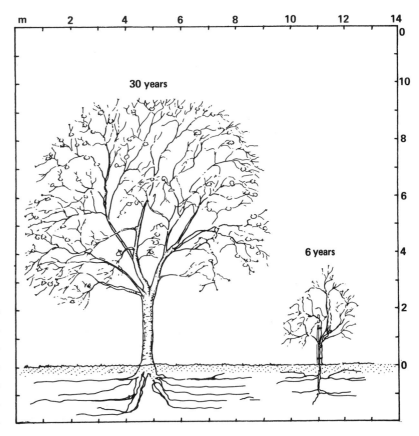

m | 2 | 4 | 6 | 8 | 10 | 12 | 14

30 years

6 years

Ptelea trifoliata – RUTACEAE
Hop Tree

Origin   North America.
A hardy deciduous tree.

Uses
This tree makes an unusual and picturesque specimen, suitable for the smaller garden.

Description
Dimensions   Average ultimate size 4.5–6m (15–20ft) high by about the same wide.
Rate of growth   Slow.
Life span   40 years or more.
Habit   Trees are short and round-headed, in some cases broader than they are high. The short, thick trunks, often leaning at an angle, are a point of interest.
Leaves   Trifoliate, green, turning yellow in autumn.
Flowers   Greenish-white and not very significant to look at, but with a strong, honeysuckle-like scent. Produced in clusters in summer.
Fruits   Oval or rounded with a circular wing, borne in profusion in autumn. When they are crushed they emit a strong, bitter scent, and it was the suggested resemblance of this smell to that of hops that led to the tree's popular name.
Bark   Dark grey-brown.

Features
The fragrance of this tree more than makes up for any shortage of colour. Until *P. trifoliata* has been more widely grown and tried it would be unwise to comment other than tentatively on its wind-firmness and other qualities.
Pollution   Fairly tolerant.
Non-poisonous.

Variety
Ptelea trifoliata 'Aurea'. An attractive yellowish-leaved form.

Requirements
Position   This tree would appear to be more suited to continental-type climates, with hot summers. It seems to do best in a sheltered, sunny situation in a warm or mild district.
Soil   A well drained, light to medium loam that is about neutral, with a pH level of 6.8–7 supports flowering and fruiting trees without apparent problems.

Notes on culture
Planting   Small trees may be planted from autumn to spring, but preferably in autumn. Stake and tie all trees at planting time and support them until they are firmly rooted.
Space   Allow each tree a minimum area of 4.5 (15ft) diameter and a similar distance from buildings.
Pruning   This consists of regulating growth to form a well shaped crown. Apart from removing poorly placed shoots little pruning is needed subsequently.

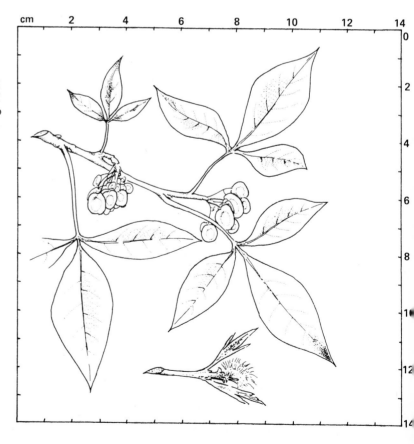

Underplanting Ground-cover plants and bulbs can be used to good effect under this tree.
Pest and disease control No serious ailments appear to trouble the Hop Tree.
Propagation By layering in autumn; or by cuttings taken in late summer. May also be increased by seeds sown in spring, but germination rates are notoriously low.

Season of interest	Winter	Spring	Late spring	Summer	Late summer	Autumn
In full leaf			X━━━━━━━━━━━━━━━━━			━X
Autumn colour						
Flowers			X━━X			
Fruits						X
Bark and stem						

The following five characteristics determine to a great extent the amount of attention a specific tree requires.

	When planted	5 years	20 years
Height	1·2 m	2·5 m	4·0 m
Width	450 mm	1·2 m	4·0 m
Root spread		2·0 m	5·0 m
Hardiness	C	B/C	B/C
Wind-firm		2	1/2

Plant care profile

	Minimum	Average	High
Site needs		X━━━━X	
Soil needs		X	
Pruning	X━━━━X		
Staking		X	
Maintenance		X	

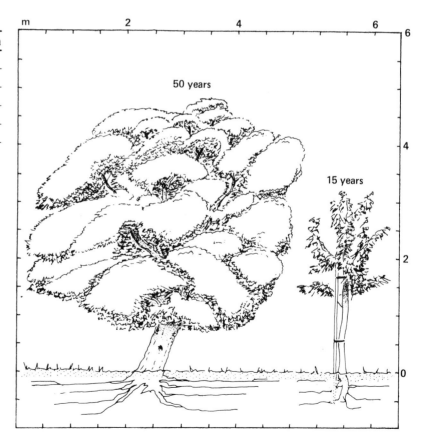

Pyrus salicifolia – ROSACEAE
Willow-leaf Pear, Grey-leaf Pear

Origin   South-eastern Europe and Western Asia.
A hardy deciduous tree.

Uses
The Willow-leaf Pear is valuable for planting in gardens, open spaces and residential areas. It is seen to best advantage when grown as a single specimen on grass. The fruits are of little use.

Description
Dimensions   Average ultimate size approximately 6–7.5m (20–25ft) high by 4.5–6m (15–20ft) wide.
Rate of growth   Slow in the early stages, increasing to moderate.
Life span   This tree can be expected to live for 70 years or more.
Habit   A tree with a broadly rounded crown.
Leaves   Long, narrow, pendulous silvery-grey leaves from late spring to autumn.
Flowers   Single white flowers which appear in clusters in spring.
Fruits   Greenish-yellow, typically pear-shaped fruits are produced in good years.
Bark   Brownish-grey.

Features
The foliage is the chief attraction of this tree, but the white flowers can be eye-catching. *P. salicifolia* is wind-firm and hardy.
Pollution   Fairly tolerant.
Non-poisonous.

Variety
Pyrus salicifolia 'Pendula'. An outstanding weeping form with drooping grey-white foliage.

Requirements
Position   The Willow-leaf Pear can be successfully grown in most cool or mild lowland districts of the temperate zone, and is suitable for use near the coast as well as inland. High ground is better avoided, however, especially in cold districts. Ideally this tree should be given a position with a south or south-westerly aspect, in full sun or lightly shaded for part of the day only, and sheltered from north and east winds.
Soil   This should be well drained and either neutral or near-neutral, pH 6.8–7, or over chalk. A deep medium loam is best, but moderately stiff or heavy loams are tolerated.

Notes on culture
Planting   Trees up to 3m (10ft) high can be planted from autumn to spring. Stake and tie all trees until they are firmly rooted.
P.s. 'Pendula' needs tying and supporting until the central leader has been trained to the required height.
Space   Allow 7.5m (25ft) diameter space for development and at least 4.5m (15ft) from buildings.
Pruning   Careful thinning and cutting is needed to form a well shaped crown, but thereafter little is necessary beyond routine maintenance pruning.
Underplanting   This tree produces fairly pendulous shoots that tend to hang down, making it unsuitable for underplanting.

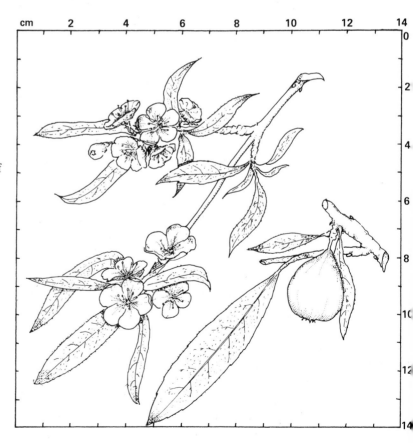

Pest and disease control Most of the pests that affect Pears can attack this tree, but the most common are aphids, various caterpillars and pear leaf blister mite. This last can cause leaf blotches. All of these can be controlled by spraying with fenitrothion if severe outbreaks occur. Canker, causing sunken areas on the stem or branches, and scab, appearing as dark spots on the leaves, are two of the more common ailments. Cut out cankered branches and check scab with captan sprays.

Propagation Usually by grafting in spring or budding in summer on the Common Pear or Quince A rootstock. Layering can be carried out in autumn, but when this tree is grown on its own roots extra attention is needed to train a straight central stem.

Season of interest	Winter	Spring	Late spring	Summer	Late summer	Autumn
In full leaf			X━━━━━━		━━━━	X
Autumn colour						
Flowers			X			
Fruits					X	
Bark and stem						

The following five characteristics determine to a great extent the amount of attention a specific tree requires.

	When planted	5 years	20 years
Height	2·4 m	3·5 m	4·5 m
Width	750 mm	2·5 m	4·0 m
Root spread		3·5 m	5·0 m
Hardiness	A/B	A/B	A/B
Wind-firm		2	1/2

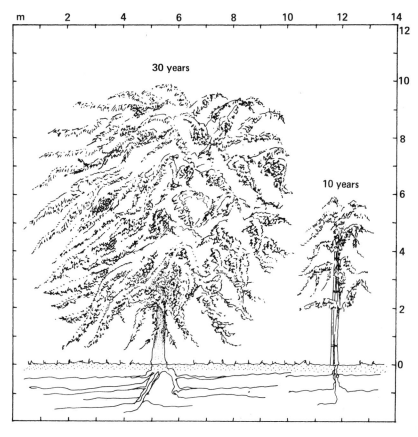

Plant care profile

	Minimum Average High
Site needs	X━━━━X
Soil needs	X
Pruning	X━━━━X
Staking	X
Maintenance	X━━━━X

119

Quercus coccinea – FAGACEAE
Scarlet Oak

Origin   North America.
A very hardy deciduous tree.

Uses
This Oak is suitable for planting on large lawns or in large shrubberies as a specimen. It is planted, either singly or in groups, in open spaces around residential areas.

Description
Dimensions   Average ultimate size 7.5–10.5m (25–35ft) high by 3–4.5m (10–15ft) wide, but exceptional trees can reach over twice that size.
Rate of growth   Moderate in early years, but slows down after 15–20 years.
Life span   In excess of 150 years.
Habit   Trees are upright at first, spreading and filling out with age.
Leaves   Green during summer, turning to crimson and scarlet shades in autumn and persisting on the lower branches until well into winter.
Flowers   Greenish catkins are the male, the female being quite inconspicuous.
Fruits   Acorns.
Bark   Rugged, greyish when mature.

Features
The colourful autumn foliage is the main attraction, but the stature and proportions of mature trees are quite impressive. The Scarlet Oak is wind-firm and frost-hardy. Its chief disadvantage for those with small gardens is its ultimate size.
Pollution   Moderately tolerant.
Non-poisonous.

Variety
Quercus coccinea 'Splendens'. The outstanding Scarlet Oak, producing particularly brilliant autumn colouring in crimsons, scarlets and yellows.

Requirements
Position   Given suitable site and soil, the Scarlet Oak can be planted in most parts of the cool or mild temperate zone, including coastal districts. A sunny situation, preferably sheltered from the north and east, will suit it best. This tree will tolerate light shade for part of the day in early years but needs full sun later for good autumn effects.
Soil   This should be a deep, fertile, sandy loam that remains moist in summer but is free-draining at all times. The soil reaction that produces the best overall results is usually about pH 6.5–6.8, but fairly satisfactory growth occurs on land with a pH level of 7. Soil fertility is important: old trees especially quite often suffer from starvation.

Notes on culture
Planting   Trees up to 2.5–3m (8–10ft) high can be planted between autumn and spring. Smaller trees, between 900mm and1.2m (3–4ft) high become established and grow away more rapidly than larger trees. Stake and tie all trees after planting, keeping them supported until they are root-firm.
Space   Allow a minimum area of 6m (20ft) diameter for development and the same distance from buildings.
Pruning   This mainly consists of forming a basic framework of branches. Thereafter it is necessary to remove only the odd straggling or crossing branch.

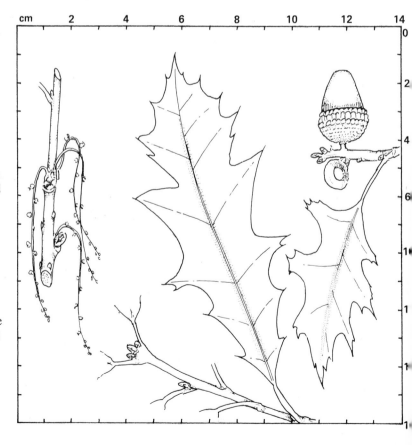

Underplanting The competition from roots of mature trees, and dry summer conditions are not conducive to good results.

Pest and disease control Oaks are unfortunately attacked by various ailments, but except for honey fungus and starvation no treatment is normally necessary. The following pests are among the most common: leaf-eating caterpillars of various insects; chafer beetles, which damage shoots by their chewing; oak gall, caused by wasp-like insects but rarely serious; oak phylloxera, forming colonies on leaf undersides and in bad cases causing premature leaf fall. Among the diseases are: various kinds of bracket fungi, usually starting on dead wood; canker and die-back, these two problems causing shoots and young branches to wither and die; mildew, occuring on the leaves as flour-like dust. Honey fungus can kill young trees. Dig out dead roots to remove possible sources or infection. Starvation is fairly common among older trees, but this need present no serious problem, as it can soon be remedied by feeding. Apply a surface top dressing in the form of a 50–75mm (2–3in) layer of a mixture of two parts soil to one part of well rotted manure or peat. Sprinkle 100g per square m (3oz per square yd) of general fertilizer over the ground before applying the top dressing.

Propagation By seeds sown in spring. Named varieties by grafting in spring on seedling *Q. coccinea.*

Plant care profile

	Minimum	Average	High
Site needs		X———X	
Soil needs		X	
Pruning	X———X		
Staking		X	
Maintenance	X———X		

Season of interest	Winter	Spring	Late spring	Summer	Late summer	Autumn
In full leaf			X———————————→X			
Autumn colour					X——→X	
Flowers			X			
Fruits					X——→X	
Bark and stem						

The following five characteristics determine to a great extent the amount of attention a specific tree requires.

	When planted	5 years	20 years
Height	1·2 m	2·0 m	5·0 m
Width	450 mm	1·2 m	2·5 m
Root spread		2·0 m	3·5 m
Hardiness	A/B	A/B	A/B
Wind-firm		1	1

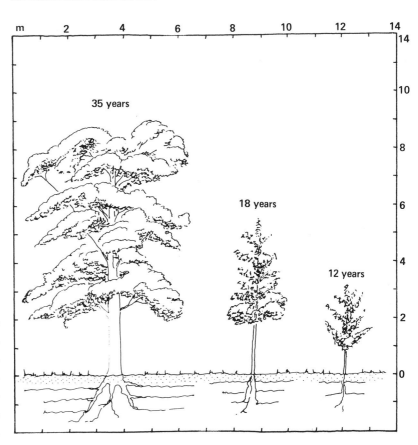

Quercus ilex – FAGACEAE
Evergreen Oak, Holm Oak

Origin   Mediterranean.
A moderately hardy evergreen tree.

Uses
As a specimen tree providing year-round interest this Oak is excellent, but as it stands trimming well and is not fast-growing it can also be used for screening. It is especially useful as a screen in coastal districts, as it is resistant to sea winds.

Description
Dimensions   Variable according to site conditions. Average ultimate size 5–7m (17–23ft) high by 4–6m (13–20ft) wide, but in good conditions it can double these figures.
Rate of growth   Usually slow.
Life span   200 years or more.
Habit   This tree forms a dense, rounded head, which becomes spreading and pendulous with increasing years.
Leaves   A pleasing dark glossy green on the upper surface and grey and felty on the underside. The foliage does produce colour all year round.
Flowers   Pendulous greenish catkins in late spring.
Fruits   Acorns in autumn.
Bark   Attractively corrugated bark which becomes progressively rougher.

Features
The leaves are the principal attraction, providing year-round greenery, and changing scenery. In gusts of wind the green upper surfaces give way to the grey of leaf undersides and vice versa. This Oak is sturdy, wind-firm and in most respects a first-class garden tree. One possible drawback is the tendency to shed old leaves in summer.
Pollution   Fairly tolerant, but inclined to grow more slowly in industrial areas.
Non-poisonous.

Varieties
Variations occur in seed-raised stock from the characteristic round-headed type to trees of more upright habit. One named variety, with narrower, dark glossy green leaves which have wavy edges is *Quercus ilex* 'Fordii'.

Requirements
Position   The Holm Oak needs a warm or a mild temperate lowland climate. Given these conditions both inland and coastal districts are suitable. An open, sunny site is ideal, but light shade is tolerated if protected from freezing winter winds.

Soil   Warm, light, deep, well drained but moisture-retentive loams suit this Oak best. A pH of 6.8–7 is ideal, but this tree also grows well over chalk.

Notes on culture
Planting   Small trees, preferably not more than 0.6–1.2m (2–4ft) in height, may be planted in autumn or spring. Stake and tie trees at planting and support until well rooted. Protect autumn-planted trees from freezing winds and cold. Water the trees, especially spring-planted ones, during the first season if necessary.

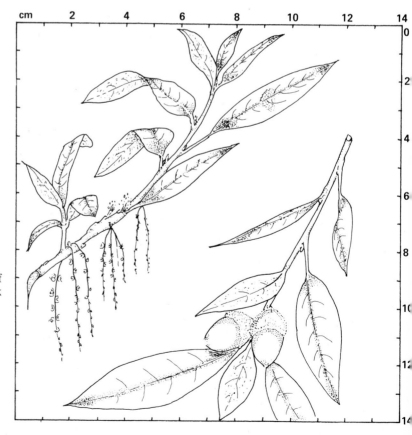

Space Allow single specimen trees minimum area of 4.5m (15ft) diameter for development, or half for trees for screening and at least 6m (20ft) from any buildings. Trees may ultimately outgrow this space, but it will be after the lifetime of the planter and probably existing buildings too.

Pruning Prune young trees to form a basic framework of branches, and remove branches as necessary to provide a clear stem. Misplaced shoots, damaged or diseased growths can be cut out in spring or autumn and the foliage, which stands cutting, can be clipped back in spring or autumn.

Underplanting The evergreen foliage and dense cover render this practice unsatisfactory with this tree.

Pest and disease control As Q. coccinea.

Propagation By seeds sown in spring. Named varieties by indoor grafting in spring on seedling stocks.

Season of interest	Winter	Spring	Late spring	Summer	Late summer	Autumn
In full leaf	X————					————X
Autumn colour						
Flowers			X			
Fruits					X——	—X
Bark and stem						

The following five characteristics determine to a great extent the amount of attention a specific tree requires.

	When planted	5 years	20 years
Height	600mm - 1·2 m	2·0 m	5·0 m
Width	400 mm	1·2 m	2·0 m
Root spread		2·0 m	3·0 m
Hardiness	C	B/C	B/C
Wind-firm		1/2	1/2

Plant care profile

	Minimum Average High
Site needs	X———X
Soil needs	X———X
Pruning	X———X
Staking	X———X
Maintenance	X

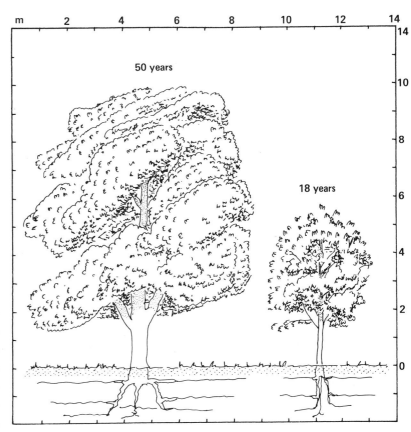

50 years

18 years

Quercus rubra – FAGACEAE
Red Oak, Northern Red Oak

Origin   North America.
A hardy deciduous tree.

Uses
Q. rubra and its varieties make very effective specimen trees, but with the exception of *Q. rubra* 'Aurea' they are best reserved for the larger garden.

Description
Dimensions   Average ultimate size 7.5–10.5m (25–35ft) high by 4.5–6.5m (15–22ft) wide, but under ideal conditions the eventual size can be half as much again.
Rate of growth   Moderate in early years but subsequently becomes slow.
Life span   This Oak comes to maturity more rapidly than many, but it can live for 150 years or more.
Habit   Trees are upright when young, but soon develop a more spreading crown.
Leaves   Larger and bolder than those of other Oaks and usually lobed. In summer they are dark green and smooth on the upper surface, dull and slightly hairy on the lower side; in autumn they turn a reddish or yellowish brown.
Flowers   Male green catkins and insignificant female flowers occur in the spring.
Fruits   Acorns produced in autumn in good years.
Bark   Grey and ultimately rugged.

Features
The Red Oak is among the quickest-growing of Oaks and is hardy, handsome and wind-firm. The leaves are the main feature of this tree.
Pollution   Fairly tolerant.
Non-poisonous.

Varieties
Quercus rubra   'Aurea'. A small- to medium-sized tree, yellow-leaved and colourful, much less vigorous than the type and not so hardy.

Requirements
Position   A cool temperate climate suits *Q. rubra,* and an open, sunny situation in a lowland area encourages good autumn colouring and larger trees. *Q. rubra* 'Aurea' needs a sheltered, sunny spot in a mild or warm district.
Soil   Ideally this should be a medium, well drained loam that is slightly acid to neutral, pH 6.5–7.

Notes on culture
Planting   Small trees, not more than 1.5–1.8m (5–6ft) high, should be planted from autumn to spring. Mulch trees after planting in hot, dry situations. Stake and tie all trees over 1m (3⅓ft) high at planting time and support until firmly rooted.
Space   Allow a minimum area of 7.5m (25ft) diameter for development and the same distance from buildings. These measurements can be reduced by one-third for the weaker-growing *Q.r.* 'Aurea'.

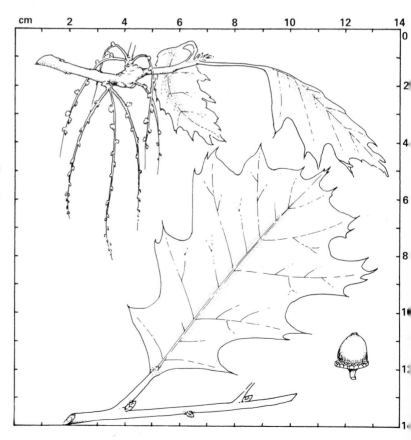

Pruning Remove misplaced and overcrowded weak branches to form a well shaped crown. Subsequently little treatment is needed, other than a little trimming to keep it in shape, and the cutting out of dead, diseased or damaged shoots.

Underplanting This practice is not particularly successful with this tree.

Pest and disease control As *Q. coccinea.*

Propagation By seed sown in autumn, within two months of the seed's being harvested. Named varieties by grafting on seedling stocks in spring.

Season of interest	Winter	Spring	Late spring	Summer	Late summer	Autumn
In full leaf			X——————X			
Autumn colour					X———X	
Flowers			X—X			
Fruits					X———X	
Bark and stem						

The following five characteristics determine to a great extent the amount of attention a specific tree requires.

	When planted	5 years	20 years
Height	1·2 m	2·0 m	5·0 m
Width	450 mm	1·5 m	2·5 m
Root spread		2·5 m	3·5 m
Hardiness	A	A	A
Wind-firm		1	1

Plant care profile

	Minimum	Average	High
Site needs		X——————X	
Soil needs		X	
Pruning	X		
Staking		X	
Maintenance	X——————X		

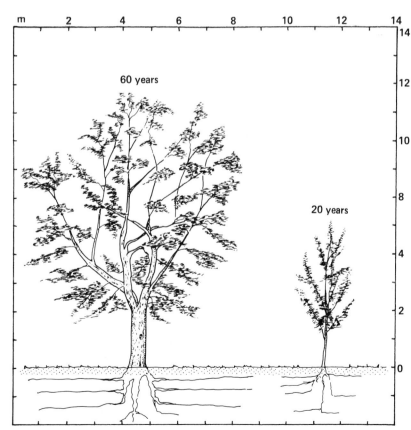

Robinia pseudoacacia – LEGUMINOSAE
Acacia, False Acacia, Locust Tree

Origin   Eastern North America. A hardy deciduous tree.

Uses
R. pseudoacacia, planted singly or in groups, makes a decorative amenity tree. It is excellent as a specimen tree, suitable for town gardens, housing estates and parkland.

Description
Dimensions   Average size at maturity 10–13m (33–43ft) high by 4–6m (13–20ft) wide. Exceptional trees can double these dimensions.
Rate of growth   Rapid to moderate.
Life span   Trees up to 100–120 years old are not uncommon.
Habit   An attractive upright tree, with rough, twisted branches.
Leaves   Dainty pinnate foliage casting medium dappled shade, but no noticeable autumn colouring.
Flowers   Long clusters of whitish pea-like flowers produced in summer.
Fruits   Seeds produced in pods like peas, appearing in late summer or autumn.
Bark   Charcoal grey.

Features
The dainty leaves and flowers are attractive, but like Silver Birch, the lightness of the foliage enables trees to be planted where others of more dense habit would be impractical or out of the question.
Pollution   Resistant.
Non-poisonous.

Varieties
Robinia pseudoacacia 'Bessoniana'. A form with an open, rounded habit.
Robinia pseudoacacia 'Frisia'. A rounded habit and golden-yellow leaves. More tender than the type.
Robinia pseudoacacia 'Inermis'. A mop-headed small tree.

Robinia pseudoacacia 'Pyramidalis'. A misnomer of fastigiate habit, columnar rather than pyramidal.
Robinia pseudoacacia semperflorens. Rounded habit. More floriferous and smaller than the type.

Requirements
Position   A lowland situation in a warm or mild temperate area will suit this tree. It should be given a position with a sunny aspect but can tolerate some shade, sheltered from east and prevailing winds and facing south or west.
Soil   This should be a well drained medium loam. *R. pseudoacacia* prefers an acid pH 6.3–6.8 to a neutral soil, but will tolerate pH 5.5–7.5.

Notes on culture
Planting   Trees up to 3m (10ft) high should be planted from autumn to spring. Stake until 4m (13ft) high.
Space   Allow 9m (30ft) diameter space and a further 4.5m (15ft) from buildings.
Pruning   Prune when young to shape the tree, cut out branches which are nearly parallel with the main stem. Thereafter only minimal trimming will be necessary to preserve the outline.

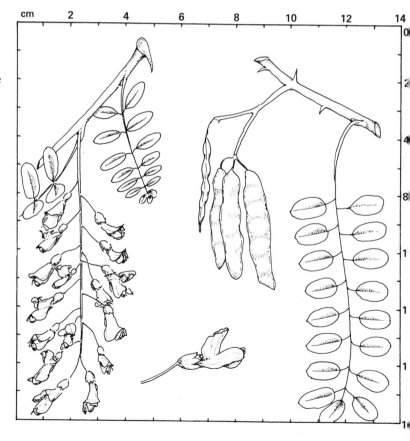

Underplanting These trees may be underplanted with shrubs, as they cast only light shade and the roots are not too exhausting.
Pest and disease control Given average care, not usually necessary.
Propagation By seeds sown in spring or suckers taken in autumn or spring. Named varieties by grafting on seedling stocks in spring.

Season of interest	Winter	Spring		Late spring	Summer		Late summer	Autumn
In full leaf				X———————————————X				
Autumn colour								
Flowers					X			
Fruits							X	
Bark and stem	X———————————————————————————————X							

The following five characteristics determine to a great extent the amount of attention a specific tree requires.

	When planted	5 years	20 years
Height	2·4 m	5·0 m	8·0 m
Width	750 mm	3·0 m	5·0 m
Root spread		4·0 m	6·0 m
Hardiness	B/C	B/C	B/C
Wind-firm		2	1/2

Plant care profile

	Minimum	Average	High
Site needs		X———X	
Soil needs		X	
Pruning	X———X		
Staking		X	
Maintenance	X———X		

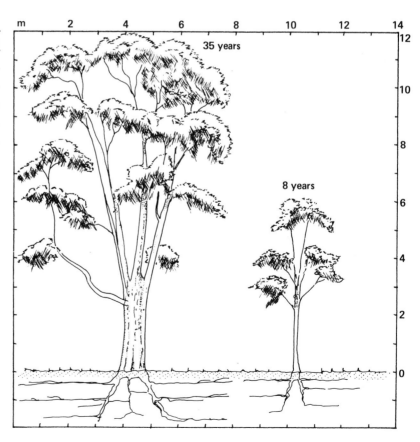

Salix matsudana – SALICACEAE
Pekin Willow

Origin   China.
A hardy deciduous tree.

Uses
These trees lend themselves to a variety of uses, as specimen trees in grass, in shrubberies, by water margins, in public gardens, open spaces or residential areas.

Description
Dimensions   Average ultimate size 6–9m (20–30ft) high by 4.5–6m (15–20ft) wide. Under ideal conditions trees can grow half as high again.
Rate of growth   Rapid to moderate.
Life span   Although the Pekin Willow has been planted more widely only this century, judging from various trees 40–50 years old the life span would appear to be well in excess of these figures.
Habit   A broadly pyramidal tree with a graceful outline.
Leaves   Long, narrow, grey-green leaves, yellowing only slightly before leaves fall.
Flowers   Yellowish-green catkins in spring. The male trees produce the longer catkins.
Fruits   Inconspicuous.
Bark   Greenish-brown.

Features
During winter the slender, leafless branches can be particularly attractive when seen against the sky. In summer, the light foliage and shoots move with every breeze. This tree is wind-firm and fairly tolerant of varying soil and site conditions.
Pollution   Tolerant.
Non-poisonous.

Varieties
Salix matsudana 'Pendula'. Similar to *S. babylonica,* the Weeping Willow, but makes a smaller, more compact tree.
Salix matsudana 'Tortuosa'. More upright and stiff in habit. The young growths are twisted and contorted.

Requirements
Position   The Pekin Willow can safely be planted in suitable sites in most lowland areas of the warm or mild temperate zone. The varieties are slightly less hardy than the type and are to be seen at their best in warm districts. A sunny or lightly shaded spot that is sheltered from late spring frosts or freezing winds will suit best.
Soil   Ideally this should be a deep, moist, medium loam that is slightly acid to neutral, having a pH of 6.8–7. The Pekin Willow grows well around pool margins but will also tolerate quite dry soils.

Notes on culture
Planting   Trees up to 3m (10ft) high should be planted between autumn and spring. Stake and tie all trees after planting and keep them supported and tied until they are well rooted.
Space   Allow a minimum area of 5m (17ft) diameter for development and at least 6m (20ft) from buildings.
Pruning   Initially the aim is to form a well shaped framework of branches, subsequently to ensure the production of replacement new wood. Cut out dead or surplus branches between autumn and spring.

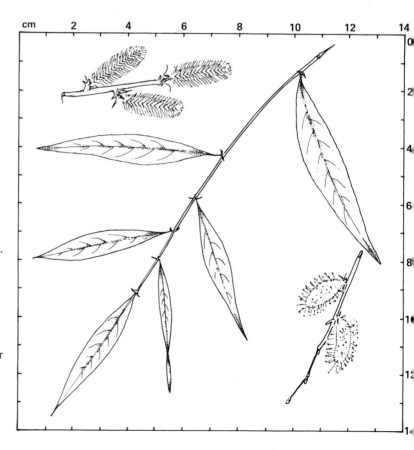

Underplanting Ground cover and bulbs can be used, but need carefully choosing to avoid spoiling the effect of the tree.

Pest and disease control Aphids are never far away; caterpillars of several moths will devour the leaves; willow scale, which occurs as whitish encrustations on the stems, considerably weakens plants. However, all these pests can be controlled by diazinon sprays. Willow anthracnose or leaf spot not only disfigures, but can seriously weaken trees. Copper-based or other fungicides can be used to keep it in check.

Propagation By hardwood cuttings in late autumn. Named varieties by budding in summer or grafting in spring on stocks of *S. matsudana.*

Plant care profile

	Minimum	Average	High
Site needs		X	
Soil needs		X	
Pruning	X——X		
Staking	X——X		
Maintenance		X	

Season of interest	Winter	Spring	Late spring	Summer	Late summer	Autumn
In full leaf			X◄————		———►X	
Autumn colour						
Flowers		X——X				
Fruits						
Bark and stem	—————	X				X-

The following five characteristics determine to a great extent the amount of attention a specific tree requires.

	When planted	5 years	20 years
Height	2·4 m	4·5 m	9·0 m
Width	900 mm	2·5 m	4·5 m
Root spread		3·5 m	5·5 m
Hardiness	B/C	B/C	B/C
Wind-firm		1/2	1

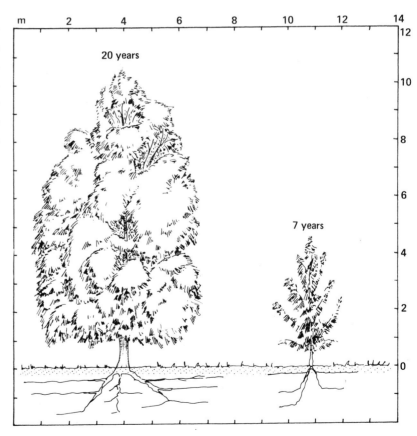

129

Sorbus aria – ROSACEAE
Common Whitebeam

Origin   Europe (including Britain). A very hardy deciduous tree.

Uses
These trees are primarily ornamental and shade trees, but they do provide particularly attractive food for birds and animal life. The Whitebeam makes an excellent specimen tree on lawns or in shrubberies, either singly or in groups of two or more.

Description
Dimensions   Average ultimate size 6–7.5m (20–25ft) high by 3–4.5m (10–15ft) wide.
Rate of growth   Moderate for the first two years, slowing down considerably with age.
Life span   In reasonable conditions 50 years and over.
Habit   A tree with a fairly upright crown, which broadens and fills out with increasing age.
Leaves   On opening in late spring the leaves are grey on the upper surface and white on the lower. Later the grey gives way to green and in autumn the leaves turn to shades of dull crimson and red.
Flowers   Clusters of fragrant white flowers appear in late spring and summer.
Fruits   Crimson-scarlet berries in late summer.
Bark   Dark greyish-brown.

Features
The Common Whitebeam is a first-class garden tree. In addition to its appeal by way of flowers, foliage and fruit it makes a safe, wind-firm tree, and the fruits are harmless.
Pollution   Resistant.
Non-poisonous.

Varieties
Sorbus aria   'Chrysophylla'. Yellowish-green leaves.
Sorbus aria   'Decaisneana'. Taller and wider than the type, and with larger leaves and fruits.
Sorbus aria   'Lutescens'. A narrower, more erect tree than the type.
Sorbus aria   'Pendula'. A rather pleasing tree of weeping habit.

Requirements
Position   The Common Whitebeam can be grown in most parts of the temperate zone, at the coast and in towns. It prefers an open, sunny situation but will tolerate light shade.

Soil   A well drained, medium or light loam that is neutral or chalky, with a pH of around 7, is ideal, but can tolerate a pH range of 6–7.5.

Notes on culture
Planting   Trees up to 3m (10ft) high should be planted between autumn and spring. Stake and tie all trees after planting, supporting them until established.
Space   Allow a minimum area of 4.5m (15ft) diameter for most varieties, and increase this to 6m (20ft) for *S.a.* 'Decaisneana'. Trees should be at least 4.5 (15ft) from buildings.

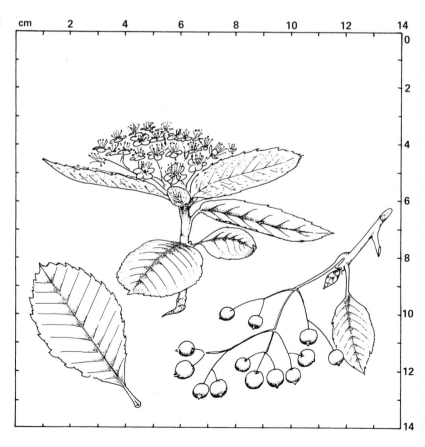

Pruning This chiefly consists of developing an initial well spaced framework of branches. Later requirements are negligible, little is necessary beyond removing any crossing or diseased branches.

Underplanting Although this tree allows shrub growth beneath its branches in the early years, as the canopy thickens and increases with age plants and shrubs may suffer. This is especially the case with *S.a.* 'Decaisneana'.

Pest and disease control The chief pests are berry-eating birds and leaf-eating caterpillars. However, they do not usually constitute a serious problem, and it is rarely necessary to resort to control measures. Among the diseases are: canker, which causes sunken areas in branches of stems; fireblight, causing shoots and leaves to wither and blacken as if burnt, rust; silver leaf; and honey fungus. Dead trees and stumps should be dug up and burnt to remover possible sources of honey fungus infection. To check the other diseases cut out any dead and diseased branches and burn.

Propagation By seeds sown in spring or autumn; or layering in autumn. Named varieties by grafting in spring or budding in summer on seedling rootstocks of *S. aucuparia,* or *Crataegus monogyna.*

Season of interest	Winter	Spring	Late spring	Summer	Late summer	Autumn
In full leaf			X———————————————————X			
Autumn colour					X———————X	
Flowers			X—X			
Fruits				X———————————————X		
Bark and stem						

The following five characteristics determine to a great extent the amount of attention a specific tree requires.

	When planted	5 years	20 years
Height	2·4 m	3·5 m	5·0 m
Width	600 mm	2·0 m	4·0 m
Root spread		3·0 m	5·0 m
Hardiness	A	A	A
Wind-firm		1	1

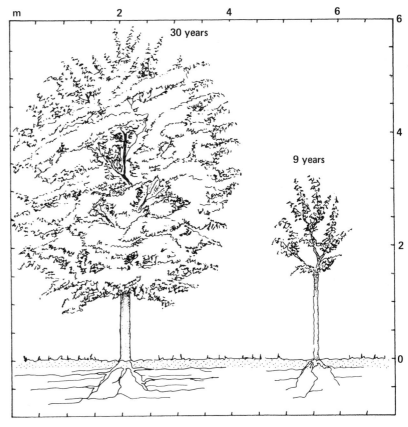

Plant care profile

	Minimum Average High
Site needs	X————X
Soil needs	X
Pruning	X
Staking	X
Maintenance	X

131

Sorbus aucuparia – ROSACEAE
Mountain Ash, Rowan, European Mountain Ash

Origin Europe (including Britain) and Western Asia.
A very hardy deciduous tree.

Uses
These trees lend themselves admirably to use as single specimens, in shrubberies and in groups of two or more.

Description
Dimensions Average ultimate size 6–9m (20–30ft) high by 3–4m (10–13ft) wide.
Rate of growth Moderate when young, slow in old age or if grown on chalk.
Life span Varies between about 30 and 70 years, the short-lived trees being found on chalk soils.
Habit In outline the tree varies from round-headed to upright.
Leaves Dainty, green, pinnate leaves, casting only light shade. In autumn they turn to bright yellow and orange, contrasting well with the bright-coloured berries.
Flowers White, fragrant flowers, appearing in clusters during late spring and early summer.
Fruits Scarlet-crimson berries that ripen in flattened clusters in late summer and autumn.
Bark Greenish-grey.

Features
The bright scarlet-crimson of the berries in summer and autumn is outstanding even among other berrying trees.
The Mountain Ash is usually well rooted and wind-firm. The fruits are harmless.
Pollution Tolerant.
Non-poisonous.

Varieties
Sorbus aucuparia ‘Asplenifolia’. An attractive tree with deeply cut, fern-like leaves.
Sorbus aucuparia ‘Beissneri’. Pinnately lobed leaf stalks and distinctive red leaf stalks.
Sorbus aucuparia ‘Fastigiata’. An upright, narrow, pyramidal more than fastigiate as the name suggests.
Sorbus aucuparia ‘Pendula’. A weeping form, makes a low, spreading tree.
Sorbus aucuparia ‘Xanthocarpa’. Orange-yellow fruits.

Requirements
Position The Mountain Ash can be planted almost anywhere in the cool temperate zone, including both towns and coastal districts. It does best in an open situation, sunny or in light shade, in an area of high rainfall. Trees on high ground or windy sites may be stunted unless they are protected from the prevailing or north and east winds.
Soil Well drained, light, sandy soils or loams that are acid or slightly acid, pH 6–6.5, suit this tree well. It tends to develop more slowly and be less long-lived on chalky soil.

Notes on culture
Planting Trees up to 3–3.5m (10–12ft) high should be planted between autumn and spring. Stake and tie all trees and support until firmly established.
Space Allow single specimen trees a minimum area of 4m (13ft) diameter. Trees in groups can be planted closer, at 2m (7ft) apart. In either case allow at least 4m (13ft) from buildings.
Pruning This mainly consists of thinning out surplus shoots to form a good crown on young trees. Subsequently little is required other than removing crossing, diseased or straggling shoots.

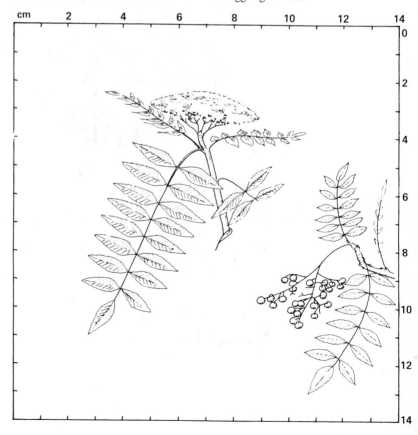

Underplanting   Heathers and heath plants can be underplanted where the shade is not too intense. Birch trees and acid-loving plants like Rhododendrons associate well with this tree.

Pest and disease control   As for *S. aria*. On alkaline or chalk soils, especially where rainfall is low, rust can be quite a problem.

Propagation   By seeds sown in autumn or spring. Named varieties by grafting in early spring or budding in summer on seedling rootstocks.

Season of interest	Winter	Spring	Late spring	Summer	Late summer	Autumn
In full leaf			X———	————	——X	
Autumn colour					X——	—X
Flowers			X—X			
Fruits					X——	—X
Bark and stem						

The following five characteristics determine to a great extent the amount of attention a specific tree requires.

	When planted	5 years	20 years
Height	2·4 m	3·0 m	6·0 m
Width	600 mm	2·5 m	4·0 m
Root spread		3·5 m	5·0 m
Hardiness	A	A	A
Wind-firm		2	1/2

Plant care profile

	Minimum	Average	High
Site needs	X———	——X	
Soil needs			X
Pruning	X		
Staking	X———	——X	
Maintenance	X		

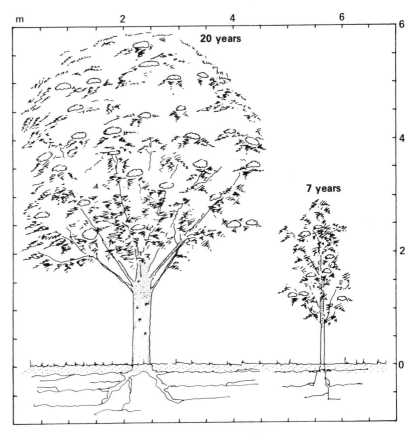

133

Sorbus hybrida – ROSACEAE
Service Tree, Bastard Service Tree

Origin Northern and Central
Europe.
A very hardy deciduous tree.

Uses
This tree is very good when planted
singly as a specimen in grass, or
among shrubs, or in groups.

Description
Dimensions Average ultimate size
6–7.5m (20–25ft) high by 3–4.5m
(10–15ft) wide.
Rate of growth Moderate initially,
slowing down after 10–12 years.
Life span Variable, but can be
expected to exceed 40 years.
Habit The branches grow upwards
to form a pyramidal crown, which
tends to become rounded or flatter
with age.
Leaves Large leaves, pinnate or
deeply lobed. Dark green in spring
and summer, they assume yellow
and reddish shades just before
falling in autumn.
Flowers Whitish flowers which
appear in late spring or early
summer in groups or flattened
clusters.
Fruits Scarlet or crimson berries
in autumn and early winter, a fine
contrast with the leaves.
Bark Brown, flecked with dark
grey. The twigs are a dark, shiny
brown in winter.

Features
The foliage of *S. hybrida* is
outstanding for leaf size and
autumn colour. The berries are
effective, either with the leaves, or
among the leafless brown shoots in
early winter. This tree is very hardy
and wind-firm. The leaf fall is quite
light, causing little or no nuisance.
Pollution Resistant.
Non-poisonous.

Varieties
Sorbus hybrida 'Fastigiata'. A
fastigiate form. Fruits well. This is
now being referred to as
S. x thuringiaca 'Fastigiata' by some
nurserymen.

Sorbus hybrida 'Gibbsii'. A form
with a more dense, compact head
or crown.

Requirements
Position This tree can be planted
almost anywhere in the cool
temperate zone, near the coast or
inland, on high ground or low. The
ideal position is an open, sunny
spot, free of shade and in an area
with a cool, moist climate. But in
warm, dry districts some light shade
for part of the day only is tolerated
without undue ill effects. Some
protection from strong winds is
desirable to ensure a well balanced
tree outline.

Soil Well drained, sandy loams
that are slightly acid to neutral, pH
6.5–7, suit this tree best. However,
slightly alkaline soils are tolerated
and *S. hybrida* can grow
satisfactorily over chalk.

Notes on culture
Planting Trees up to 3m (10ft)
high should be planted between
autumn and spring. Stake and tie
all trees over 1m (3½ft) high and
keep them supported until they are
firmly rooted.
Space Allow specimen trees a
minimum area of 4.5m (15ft)
diameter and the same distance
again from buildings.

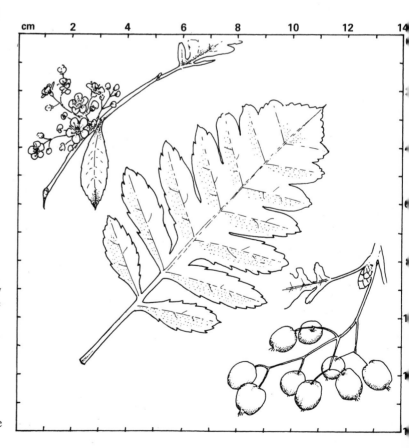

Pruning This chiefly consists of limiting young trees to a single main trunk, removing any badly placed shoots to form a well shaped crown. Subsequently little or no pruning is needed.

Underplanting Low-growing shrubs, and ground-cover plants can be used successfully beneath the branches of this tree.

Pest and disease control As for *S. aria.*

Propagation By seeds sown in autumn. Named varieties by grafting in spring or budding in summer on S. aucuparia rootstocks.

Season of interest	Winter	Spring	Late spring	Summer	Late summer	Autumn
In full leaf			X————————		—X	
Autumn colour					X———	—X
Flowers			X—X			
Fruits					X———	—X
Bark and stem						

The following five characteristics determine to a great extent the amount of attention a specific tree requires.

	When planted	5 years	20 years
Height	2·4 m	3·0 m	5·0 m
Width	450 mm	1·2 m	3·0 m
Root spread		2·0 m	4·0 m
Hardiness	A	A	A
Wind-firm		1	1

Plant care profile

	Minimum	Average	High
Site needs	X———————X		
Soil needs			X
Pruning	X		
Staking	X		
Maintenance	X		

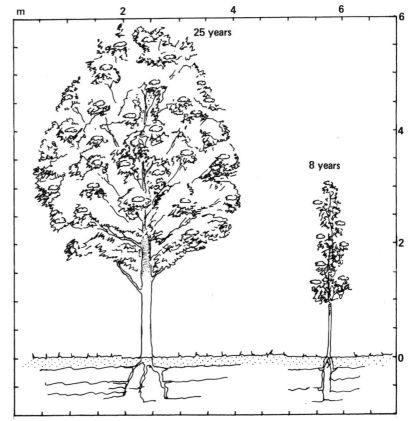

Tilia platyphyllos – TILIACEAE
Broad-leaved Lime, Big-leaf European Linden

Origin Central and Southern Europe.
A hardy deciduous tree.

Uses
This Lime is best used as a specimen tree in a large garden.

Description
Dimensions Average ultimate size 7.5–10.5m (25–35ft) high by 4.5–6m (15–20ft) wide.
Rate of growth Fairly rapid initially, decreasing to moderate. Pollarded trees, however, continue to grow rapidly.
Life span Trees mature at about 30 years old, but live for upwards of 150–200 years.
Habit A round-headed tree.
Leaves Broad, heart-shaped leaves which open mid-green and turn dark green, becoming yellow in autumn to give a mottled green and gold effect.
Flowers Yellowish-green, fragrant flowers, quite decorative when present in abundance, produced in summer.
Fruits Roughly rounded pale green and globular, not particularly conspicuous individually, but collectively give a creamy cast to the whole tree.
Bark Dark and light grey.

Features
This Lime eventually forms a stately tree. It attracts bees when in flower, and is pleasing to the eye both when in leaf and in winter. It does not usually suffer from the unsightly burrs on the trunks which often afflict *T.* x *europaea* (the Common Lime).
Pollution Resistant.
Non-poisonous.

Varieties
Tilia platyphyllos 'Aurea'. This variety has young branches which are yellowish, turning green, and paler green foliage.
Tilia platyphyllos 'Fastigiata'. A pyramidal form with upright, ascending branches is usual rather than fastigiate as the name seems to imply.
Tilia platyphyllos 'Pendula'. A weeping form.
Tilia platyphyllos 'Rubra' (Red-twigged Lime). A form with a fairly erect, upright-branching habit and brown-red shoots in winter.

Requirements
Position This Lime grows well in lowland areas of the mild temperate zone. A sunny lowland or valley site, preferably in a warm district, will suit it best. It tolerates town conditions remarkably well. Avoid very exposed planting sites.
Soil Ideally this should be a well drained medium loam that is moist, fairly deep and neutral or near-neutral, pH range 7–7.2. However, this tree will grow well on chalk or limestone where there is a fair depth of soil – 450–600mm (1½–2ft).

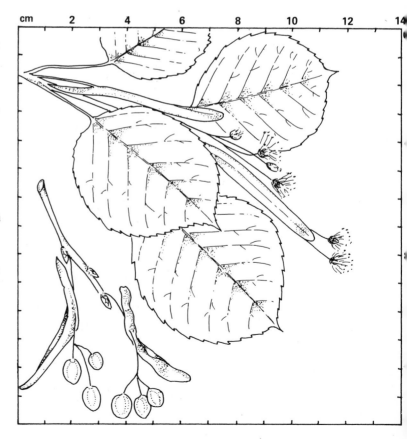

Notes on culture

Planting Trees up to 4m (13ft) high should be planted between autumn and spring. Stake and tie all trees over 1m (3⅓ft) and keep them supported until firmly rooted.

Space Allow a minimum area of 6m (20ft) diameter for each tree and the same distance from any buildings.

Pruning This chiefly consists of shortening or removing poorly placed shoots to form an initial framework of well spaced branches. Subsequently little or no pruning is needed beyond cutting out crossing or badly placed growths to maintain the shape.

Underplanting Shrubs and ground cover plants can be grown successfully under trees in sunny situations, but low-growing subjects are preferable.

Pest and disease control Aphids which cause honey dew and sooty moulds can be checked with malathion or other insecticide sprays. Caterpillars of various insects can be controlled with derris or other insecticides. Diseases such as canker and die-back are checked by cutting out affected areas. Dig out and burn dead roots to remove sources of honey fungus infection. Leaf spot can be controlled with copper or other fungicides but is rarely treated except when it occurs in young trees in the nursery.

Propagation By seeds sown in spring; or layering in autumn. Named varieties by grafting on seedling rootstocks in spring.

Plant care profile

	Minimum	Average	High
Site needs		X	
Soil needs		X	
Pruning	X———X		
Staking		X	
Maintenance	X———X		

Season of interest	Winter	Spring	Late spring	Summer	Late summer	Autumn
In full leaf			X———————		—X	
Autumn colour					X———	—X
Flowers			X—X			
Fruits					X—X	
Bark and stem	■———————		—X			X—

The following five characteristics determine to a great extent the amount of attention a specific tree requires.

	When planted	5 years	20 years
Height	2·4 m	4·5 m	7·5 m
Width	750 mm	2·5 m	6·0 m
Root spread		3·5 m	7·0 m
Hardiness	B/C	B	B
Wind-firm		1	1

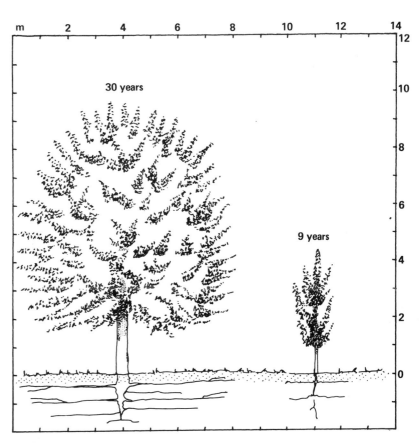

30 years

9 years

Cultivation—a summary chart

Name	Size(m) height	width	Growth rate	Planting season	Planting size
Acer campestre	6	3	slow-moderate	autumn-spring	ordinary
Acer griseum	5	2.5	slow	autumn-spring	small
Acer japonicum	6	3	moderate-slow	autumn	small
Acer negundo	7.5	4	rapid-moderate	autumn-spring	ordinary
Acer pensylvanicum	6	3.5	moderate	autumn-spring	ordinary
Acer platanoides	12	7.5	rapid-moderate-slow	autumn-spring	ordinary
Acer pseudoplatanus	12	6	rapid-moderate	autumn-spring	ordinary
Aesculus x carnea	7	4	moderate	autumn-spring	ordinary
Betula pendula	9	3.5	rapid-moderate	autumn-spring	ordinary
Carpinus betulus	8	4.5	moderate-slow	autumn-spring	ordinary
Catalpa bignonioides	7.5	6	slow	autumn	small
Cercidiphyllum japonicum	9	6.5	moderate-slow	autumn	small
Cercis siliquastrum	6	4.5	slow	autumn	small
Cotoneaster frigidus	6	4.5	rapid-moderate	autumn-spring	ordinary
Crataegus crus-galli	6	6	moderate-slow	autumn-spring	ordinary
Crataegus oxyacantha	6	5	rapid-moderate	autumn-spring	ordinary
Davidia involucrata	7	5	moderate-slow	autumn	small
Eucalyptus gunnii	12	4.5	rapid-moderate	spring	small
Fagus sylvatica	24	15	slow-moderate	autumn-spring	ordinary
Fraxinus excelsior	9	4.5	rapid-moderate	autumn-spring	ordinary
Gleditsia triacanthos	9	4.5	moderate-slow	autumn-spring	small
Koelreuteria paniculata	5	3	slow-moderate	autumn-spring	small
Laburnum anagyroides	7.5	4	slow-moderate	autumn-spring	ordinary
Liquidambar styraciflua	7.5	3.5	moderate-slow	autumn-spring	ordinary
Liriodendron tulipifera	9	4.5	rapid-moderate	autumn-spring	small
Malus hupehensis	9	6	rapid-moderate	autumn-spring	ordinary
Malus x purpurea	7.5	5	moderate-slow	autumn-spring	ordinary
Malus tschonoskii	12	4	moderate	autumn-spring	ordinary
Morus nigra	6	4.5	slow	autumn-spring	small
Parrotia persica	5	4	slow	autumn	small
Paulownia tomentosa	7.5	4.5	moderate-rapid	autumn	small
Populus alba	12	7.5	rapid-moderate	autumn-spring	ordinary
Prunus avium	12	9	rapid-moderate	autumn-spring	ordinary
Prunus cerasifera	7.5	7.5	rapid-moderate	autumn	ordinary
Prunus dulcis	7.5	7.5	rapid-moderate	autumn	ordinary
Prunus padus	9	6	moderate-rapid	autumn-spring	ordinary
Prunus persica	7.5	7.5	rapid-moderate	autumn	ordinary
Prunus serrulata	7.5	7.5	rapid-moderate	autumn-spring	ordinary

Hardiness	Maintenance needs	Soil reaction	Site and light requirements
B	low-average	NC	sun and shelter/ls
B/C	average	N	sun and shelter/ls
C	high-average	A	sun and shelter
B	average	ANC	sun and shelter
B	average	AN	sun and shelter/ls
A	low	ANC	sun and shelter/ls
A	average-low	ANC	sun and shelter
B	average-high	ANC	sun and shelter
A	low	AN	sun and shelter/ls
A	low	ANC	sun/ls
B/C	average	N	sun and shelter
B/C	average	NC	sun and shelter
C	average	NC	sun and shelter
B/C	low-average	NC	sun and shelter
A	high-average	ANC	sun and shelter/ls
A	average	ANC	sun and shelter/ls
B/C	average	AN	sun and shelter
B/C	high-average	N	sun and shelter
A	low-average	NC	sun and shelter/ls
A	low-average	NC	sun/ls
C	high-average	NC	sun and shelter/ls
C	average	N	sun and shelter
A	low-average	AN	sun and shelter/ls
B/C	high-average	N	sun and shelter/ls
B	average-low	AN	sun and shelter/ls
A	average	N	sun and shelter
A/B	average	AN	sun and shelter
A	low-average	AN	sun and shelter/ls
B/C	low-average	N	sun and shelter
B/C	average	AN	sun and shelter
C	high-average	N	sun and shelter
A/B	average	N	sun and shelter
A	low	N	sun and shelter/ls
A	average	N	sun and shelter/ls
B/C	average-high	NC	sun and shelter
A	low-average	AN	sun and shelter/ls
B/C	average	AN	sun and shelter
B	average-low	AN	sun and shelter/ls

Continued

Key to chart

Size
ultimate height and width in metres.

Growth rate
rapid   = over 300mm per year.
moderate = 150–300mm per year.
slow   = less than 150mm per year.

Planting season
when to plant.

Planting size
ordinary = trees up to 3m high.
small   = trees of 2m and less.

Hardiness
A = hardy throughout the temperate zone.
B = hardy in mild areas of the temperate zone.
C = hardy in warm areas only.

Maintenance needs
high = trees needing above average attention.
low = trees needing minimal care.

Soil reaction
trees need or will tolerate
A = acid soil. pH below 7.
N = neutral soil. pH 7.
C = chalk or alkaline soil. pH above 7.
Combinations indicate the range tolerated.

Site and light requirements
sun   = open to sun.
shelter = protection from cold or strong wind needed.
ls   = light shade tolerated.

139

Summary chart – continued

Name	Size(m)		Growth rate	Planting season	Planting size
	height	width			
Prunus subhirtella	9	7.5	moderate-rapid	autumn-spring	ordinary
Ptelea trifoliata	6	6	slow	autumn	small
Pyrus salicifolia	7.5	6	slow-moderate	autumn-spring	ordinary
Quercus coccinea	10.5	4.5	moderate-slow	autumn-spring	small
Quercus ilex	7	6	slow	autumn or spring	small
Quercus rubra	10.5	6.5	moderate-slow	autumn-spring	small
Robinia pseudoacacia	13	6	rapid-moderate	autumn-spring	ordinary
Salix matsudana	9	6	rapid-moderate	autumn-spring	ordinary
Sorbus aria	7.5	4.5	moderate-slow	autumn-spring	ordinary
Sorbus aucuparia	9	4	moderate-slow	autumn-spring	ordinary
Sorbus hybrida	7.5	4.5	moderate-slow	autumn-spring	ordinary
Tilia platyphyllos	10.5	6	rapid-moderate	autumn-spring	ordinary

Hardiness	Maintenance needs	Soil reaction	Site and light requirements
B/C	average-low	N	sun and shelter
B/C	average	AN	sun and shelter
A/B	high-average	NC	sun and shelter/ls
A/B	low-average	AN	sun and shelter/ls
B/C	average	NC	sun and shelter/ls
A	low-average	AN	sun and shelter
B/C	average-low	ANC	sun and shelter/ls
B/C	average	N	sun and shelter/ls
A	low	ANC	sun and shelter/ls
A	low	A	sun/ls
A	low	ANC	sun/ls
B	average-low	NC	sun and shelter

Glossary

Acid   having a pH level below 7.

Alkaline   having a pH level above 7.

Berry   small fleshy fruit, usually containing seeds.

Catkin   pendulous flower-spike devoid of petals.

Chlorosis   a yellowing of plant leaves usually caused by a deficiency of iron in soils.

Deciduous   shedding the leaves in winter.

Dormant   in a resting condition, used here with reference to leafless trees, shoots and seeds that are resting and not actively growing.

Fastigiate   tall, narrow and upright in habit.

Fungicide   substance used to control fungus disease.

Grafting   joining two plants together, so that one, the rootstock, acts for the other, the scion.

Half-standard   having clear unbranched trunk at least 1m and less than 1.7m from ground to lowest branches.

Hardy   able to grow outdoors and survive the winters without serious harm.

Hybrid   a tree or plant resulting from the crossing of two distinct varieties.

Insecticide   a substance used to control insect pests.

Lime   a material containing chalk or calcium compounds.

Loam   a soil containing a well balanced mixture of clay and sand, usually free-draining.

Mulch   a surface application of manure, peat or similar around tree trunks to prevent moisture loss.

Neutral   neither acid nor alkaline and having a pH level of 7.

pH   a scale of measurement used to indicate acidity or alkalinity where 7 is neutral, above is alkaline, and below is acid.

Propagation   process by which plants are increased.

Pyramidal   conical in outline, broader at the base, tapering towards the top.

Rootstock and Scion   see Grafting, above.

Standard   having clear unbranched trunk at least 1.7m from ground to lowest branch.

Stratification   a process in which seeds are subjected to cold and frost to break dormancy and assist germination.

Trunk   the main stem of a tree above the ground and below the lowest branch.

Underplanting   practice of planting low-growing subjects under or among taller trees and shrubs.

Weed   plant, usually of little use, growing in an unwanted place.

Bibliography

Bean, W. J., *Trees and Shrubs Hardy in the British Isles,* vols. I–III, Murray, London, 1970–76

Chittenden, F. J., (ed.), *The Royal Horticultural Society Dictionary of Gardening,* Oxford University Press, London, 1956

Conover, H. S., *Grounds Maintenence Handbook,* McGraw Hill, New York, 1977

Hay, R. and Beckett, K., *The Reader's Digest Encyclopedia of Garden Plants and Flowers,* Reader's Digest, London, 1975

Hilliers' Manual of Trees and Shrubs, David and Charles, Newton Abbot, 1974

Rehder, A., *Manual of Cultivated Trees and Shrubs,* Collier Macmillan, New York, 1940